JOURNEY
to an
EXPECTED
END

Michelle Ziregbe

WESTBOW·
PRESS
A DIVISION OF THOMAS NELSON
& ZONDERVAN

WestBow Press books may be ordered through booksellers or by contacting:

WestBow Press
A Division of Thomas Nelson & Zondervan
1663 Liberty Drive
Bloomington, IN 47403
www.westbowpress.com
1 (866) 928-1240

Scripture taken from the Holy Bible, NEW INTERNATIONAL VERSION®. Copyright © 1973, 1978, 1984 by Biblica, Inc. All rights reserved worldwide. Used by permission. NEW INTERNATIONAL VERSION® and NIV® are registered trademarks of Biblica, Inc. Use of either trademark for the offering of goods or services requires the prior written consent of Biblica US, Inc.

Scripture taken from the King James Version of the Bible.

Scripture taken from the New King James Version. Copyright © 1979, 1980, 1982 by Thomas Nelson, Inc. Used by permission. All rights reserved.

Scripture quotations taken from the Holy Bible, New Living Translation, Copyright © 1996, 2004. Used by permission of Tyndale House Publishers, Inc., Wheaton, Illinois 60189. All rights reserved.

ISBN: 978-1-4908-7909-3 (sc)
ISBN: 978-1-4908-7910-9 (hc)
ISBN: 978-1-4908-7908-6 (e)

Library of Congress Control Number: 2015907099

Print information available on the last page.

WestBow Press rev. date: 05/11/2015

CONTENTS

DEDICATION

I dedicate this book to God, who inspired me to write it and stood by me through all the seasons. This book is for the glory of my biggest supporter and my eternal King.

INTRODUCTION

One day, I was sitting in class and heard a voice: "If you don't use the gifts I have given you, I will take them away and give them to another." I had no doubt God was speaking, because He had been speaking to me for a while about starting a blog.

As I was trying to concentrate in a lecture room with about three hundred other students, God interrupted my thoughts to give me what I considered a final warning. If my ears had been blocked before, they were certainly open then to His prompting, especially since He was very descriptive about what would happen if I continued to disobey.

I had always had a passion for writing. As a child, I wrote plays, songs, and poems, and while everyone else asked for Barbie dolls, I asked for books. (I still got my Barbie; I just wanted my books a lot more!) But when God told me to start writing again, my mind told me blogs were too basic. I thought, *C'mon, Lord! Everyone seems to have a blog. What possible difference could I make by writing one more?*

Truth is, I was scared. I struggled with feelings of inadequacy, and I couldn't understand why God would want to use me instead of another writer. *Who will even read it, Lord? What could I possibly say that hasn't already been said?*

But when I heard His words that day, I turned on my laptop and started my first blog, "As the Spirit Leads." The name was whispered to my heart by God; He wanted to remind me He wasn't calling me because I was qualified; He wanted me to rest on His qualifications alone. He would give me His words, and all I had to do was follow His lead.

As a result of taking that leap of faith, my blog has reached people all over the globe, from the United States and Nigeria and Russia to the United Kingdom and Brazil and so many more places.

After a time, I was invited to lead Bible study at my former university a couple of times, and that opened doors for me to serve as mentor, speaker, and teacher of the Word. I realized that when you're obedient to God, He will open doors no one else could open or shut; He will take you places where fancy degrees and skills can never carry you.

The first topic I addressed on my blog had to do with gifts. In it, I urged people to be productive with the gifts God has given them. The Lord brought my attention to the story of the man in Matthew 25 who gave three of his servants gold according to their capabilities. Upon his return, he learned that one of them had buried his gold while the others had invested and multiplied theirs. The man scolded the unproductive servant and gave his gold to one of the other servants.

Later on, this chapter will tell how those who use what they have been given will experience an increase while those who do not will be thrown away as the wicked servant was. Are you a servant who puts his gold to work, or are you a servant who sits on his gold?

We all have been set apart by God; no two of us are the same. The portions allotted to each of us are measured by the capabilities the Lord has put in us. Sure, we'll find people with similar characteristics on the surface, but if we look deeper, we'll find differences. These differences cause our paths to be diverse, but they lead to the same end, and it's not here on earth. Granted, we can achieve wonderful things and attain heights on earth, but we should not confuse that with our expected end. Everything we do on earth is preparation for uniting with Jesus in heaven. If achieving earthly results was the end God had for us, He'd have no need to promise us eternity.

Have you ever felt you didn't have what it took to walk down the path God set for you? As I wrote this book, I battled with doubts that made me think my words weren't good enough and didn't matter. When I'd compare my writing with that of others, questioning the worth of the unique voice God had given me, I felt intimidated. But God spoke to me: "My people don't need fancy words; they just need the truth. Allow me to do the changing; all you need to be is the vessel."

I don't have a foreword from anyone famous, which bothered me until I realized I had something much more valuable—a calling coupled with justification from the one whose words hold the sun, moon, and stars in the sky. Even back when I was just a painting in His mind, He predestined me and set me apart for a time such as this, and that is all the endorsement I needed. And that's all you need to walk in the path He has set for you. Knowing that His seal of approval was on this project and me, I rested on His promise so I could pen *Journey to an Expected End* as He wanted.

My prayer is that the words of this book, as inspired by the Holy Spirit, will make you reassess your journey on earth and push toward your expected end. You don't have to be perfect, just willing to let God use you. With this book, I wanted to inspire the members of this generation, which God has set apart before the foundations of the earth, to learn the lessons from their experiences and move on so when He returns, they will not be found wanting.

In this book, I share my experiences, stories, practical tips, prayers, and lessons I have learned because transparency breeds community. We live in a society that teaches us how to cover our scars when in reality the scars bear a purpose much higher than we think.

I pray that as you read this book, the experiences I have been through will relate to you where you are and give you insight into the importance of the journey you are on. As you read, I pray the Lord tugs on your heart and the words provoke you to come out front and become the person He created you to be in Jesus' name!

CHAPTER 1

The Mystery of Finding Yourself

They just always seemed so sure, but I didn't have a clue. I wished I were as confident about myself as they appeared to be about themselves, but to be confident, I needed something to be confident about. Outside looking in can be very deceptive; we all have a tendency to mask who we are with false confidence, arrogance, or even pride when deep down we're at war with ourselves.

I know that not everyone needs to know our business, but sometimes, the person we're hiding from is ourselves. We have an "idea" of whom the world expects us to be, and we take on that identity rather than finding our true identity in Christ. It seems much easier to take up false identities than to endure through the process of finding ourselves. Then we try to ignore the war within us, but that won't go away until we face our fears that the person we may find might not be all that. But we are just enough!

To find ourselves, we must first seek the face of the Lord and truthfully ask Him not just to show us His face but also to give us the courage to accept it. After seeking His face, sooner or later, we will end up in what appears to be a boxing ring facing Goliath. He represents the very thing we may have run from our whole lives, that part of us we've tried to bury just so we won't have it deal with. However, it doesn't have much to do with Goliath as with exposing the content of our hearts. How do we react? What did our hearts say? Did we learn the lesson? If not, why not? It's in that ring that God shows us what we are made of and who we really are.

I was born in Nigeria; I lived there up until age fifteen before moving to England with my Mother and Brother. My parents are divorced, and I had lived with my mom a majority of my life so after about a year in England, my brother and I moved to the United States to live with my Dad. While I was getting ready to move to the States, I went to a doctor for some tests accompanied by my mom. The nurse took me into a room after asking my mom to wait outside. I put on a hospital robe, and the doctor came in and used a stethoscope to listen to my heart.

That is a pretty standard procedure, and it never takes long. Or usually not. I saw her demeanor change, but at that point, I was tired of all the tests, immunizations, meetings, and traveling, so I just let it be. But she asked me, "Are you aware you have a heart murmur?"

Though I wasn't sure what that meant, I nodded. My doctor spotted my confusion and sent for my mom. She told her about the murmur, but my mom was in disbelief. I'd been to plenty other doctors, now all of a sudden this one was talking about a murmur? The doctor said the murmur caused by a hole in my heart was very loud; it was the first thing she heard when she listened. She encouraged us to get it further examined.

When we shared this news with our family, everyone disbelieved it; they thought the doctor had heard it wrong. I saw their faith, but that didn't cut it for me. I set up a meeting with my doctor, and I googled what *murmur* meant. I ended up scared, particularly after learning some people with heart murmurs required surgery.

I soaked my pillow and cried out to God. Why a sixteen-year-old had to deal with that I didn't know. I felt as though I were hanging on by just a thin thread of faith. But that turned out to be just enough for God to work with.

As I walked to the hospital, I prayed and sang praises to God while picturing Him holding my hands. I knew He was with me and would show the Enemy that His hands were on me.

The second doctor told me he heard the noise but didn't think it was as loud and as obvious as the first doctor had thought. He recommended me to a specialist. I praised God the whole way home. He was listening and was with me, and that increased my faith in Him.

Long story short, the specialist said that there was no murmur, that my heart was perfectly fine. God truly blew my mind. He had healed me completely! After stepping into that ring to fight, I was hit hard, but I was restored, and my faith in God grew. My scar was completely healed.

But that isn't always the case. Sometimes, we have to live with the scars we get from battles we may not have known about. When I was younger, I lost all hearing in one ear due to the mumps. I never really faced many problems except when people spoke to me on the right side, but school-wise, it wasn't that bad until my later years. I've been told many times to get a hearing aid, but I'm convinced God will heal me one day. You may say, "Well, God has solved your problems by the invention of hearing aids," but I've found peace in what Jesus said in Matthew 8:13 about letting things be done according to my faith.

But then, I felt I was losing my hearing in my left ear, and on top of that, I started having breathing problems. So I was back in the boxing ring. Another doctor told me I had a heart murmur.

Pause. *Huh?* I told him there had to be a mistake. But another doctor said the same thing. It was all too much. Breathing problem? Hearing problem? And then that heart murmur? Again?

I knew the Enemy was responsible, but I remembered God had completely healed me, so I discarded the reports. Nonetheless, I went back for further screening. Regardless of what result would come back, I just knew I was healed, and it was so. A specialist told me I was cleared from my murmur and breathing problem.

In the book of Luke, we read about many people being healed—the blind, the lame, lepers, the woman with the issue of blood, and so on. They were healed according to their faith, and this principle is applicable to us today.

Such was my case as I sat on the hospital bed listening to suggestions about a cochlear transplant to correct my hearing problems. But as I wrote, my heart was (and still is) fixed on my belief that God will restore my hearing. If He doesn't, well, I believe it's still part of His plan. It's a scar I have lived with since childhood, but God told me that the Enemy sought to destroy me completely but that He had saved me. I might not have full hearing, but what I have is enough for Him to work with.

Now, when I'm faced with adversity, I know I can trust God and persevere, but I never would have known that about myself if I'd never gotten into that ring to fight. Even if you left the ring without a scratch, you can learn a lesson from your fight about the things God has put inside you. Don't run away from the ring, because as bad as it might look, not knowing is even worse. It causes you to live under a shadow of doubt. Trust me; the grass is much greener on the side of certainty.

When I find myself in turmoil, I remember times when I was in the ring, and I draw courage from my capacity for faith in God. When it seems I can't, it's not for lack of faith but because I really don't want to put in the work. That, however, doesn't change the fact that I've been equipped to handle the situation. So have you.

Practical Tips

- One way to stop comparing yourself to others is by reflecting on the fact that God uniquely sculpted you. Use the life of Jesus illustrated in the bible as your standard for comparison.
- Remember that God's word is sufficient to sustain you in the ring. Write a list of scriptures pertaining to your situation to strengthen you when you feel

weary. Recite them to yourself, and/or paste in areas that you encounter the most. For example your room door, office wall, phone screensaver, and so on.

- Try Journaling on your phone or in a book to help to keep track of the days. This way you won't miss little details that can help with understanding the lessons to be learned. Write what happened that day, how you felt, and your response.
- Take this journal to the Lord often. Ask Him to point out trends you may not have seen and give you wisdom on how to physically implement your findings.

Prayer

Lord, reveal to us the ways that we don't live according to your standard rather that which we have seen others do. Give us the grace to accept what you show us, and faith to believe that even if it's not good, You are capable of changing us. Teach us to depend on you as we learn the lessons from the ring, knowing that our hope will never fail.

CHAPTER 2

Confessions of an Ambivert

I am an extroverted introvert. That's my diagnosis of the person I have come to know better over the last couple of years. When I was younger, I could talk to anyone and was very bold in my approach and brave in my beliefs. I was a nine-year-old girl who would preach to kids on the playground to accept Jesus. But as the years went on, I began listening to voices of doom that convinced me I had nothing worth sharing.

As a result, I restricted whom I let in and when and how I did. When I meet new people, I am reserved. I prefer meeting people in groups; that way, I can scope out any one person from the outside looking in.

People said I was standoffish, but underneath, I was just a girl who tried to mask her insecurities because she was afraid people would see through her. I found it hard to accept myself; I wasn't comfortable in my own skin. I never thought I was good enough, pretty enough, or smart enough. I thought maybe if I tried what everyone else was doing, I could at least blend, but I was so wrong. I can still look standoffish, but that's a force of habit; it isn't because

I think I'm better. It's a by-product of low self-esteem airbrushed with forced confidence.

We are so quick to jump to conclusions about people. Just by reading the last few pages of this book, I'm sure you have an image of me. But I challenge you to read this whole book and look under the surface a little deeper next time you meet someone. You may be surprised to find he or she is cool, but you'll never know if you don't push past the front cover.

I'm one of those who pretend to be on the phone when I get nervous and want to avoid eye contact. I've learned the importance of simply looking up. That spirit of timidity is not of the Lord. We have been given the spirit of boldness and of sound minds. Your Father is a lion in whose image you were created; you can be brave as well.

Boldness, however, comes from a heart content in God's ability, not its inability. The only time you should look down is when you bow to worship God. Silence the voice of the Enemy that causes you to hide in the background.

In ourselves, we are nothing, but when we have Christ in us and let His light shine through, we can be compared to the sun. Our rays bring hope that says darkness is but for a moment. We should all come out of our shells so we can be the best God has created us to be.

My extroverted half comes out when I know a person. Sometimes, I talk so much to others, even those I have just met, and they can't get a word out. Maybe I talk so much so they won't have time to process what I said and find fault with it. Maybe it's so I can say something that seems worthy of being heard.

These traits for my introverted and extroverted sides stem from the same problem — discontentment. Comparison is the enemy of progress. When we aren't comfortable with ourselves, we find ways to cope, but that puts us in bondage. We spend too much time talking ourselves up to gain approval or hiding to avoid confronting who we are. This derails us from what God intended for us—to go into the world even though we are not of it and be a light to people.

We cannot influence people if we can't accept ourselves. The people God has called us to reach most times are different from us, so how could we reach them if all we see is our insecurity reflected in their faces?

We are most comfortable with people who look like us and have things in common with us because we think we're on the same plane with them. Interacting with someone who looks different may cause us to realize what we lack. We are the salt of the earth, and salt gives seasoning. When you add the same seasoning to all food, it ends up tasting the same, whereas different mixes of seasonings can impart each dish a unique flavor. God created us as unique "seasonings" to flavor others' lives and the world at large.

Some people are naturally introverted or extroverted; that isn't bad unless they hinder our doing what God wants us to do. I know that introverts need to stand back and observe a bit before we make our moves, but sometimes, God needs us to act immediately to show others His life-changing powers. And I understand extroverts' need to speak their minds and their love of talking, but we extroverts are at times supposed to just listen to show people the love of God. It doesn't matter which category we fall into, we should

9

be content in God and not let any "grouping" stop us from moving when God tells us to.

Practical Tips

- The first step to overcoming shyness and timidity is to ask God to give you confidence in yourself. Believing you have something worth sharing replaces anxiousness with boldness. If you are an extrovert who tends to "overshine" others, ask God to give you an inner peace that will not be swayed by what you feel are your shortcomings. Ask Him to give you confidence to receive others without trying to prove yourself.
- Learn to smile when someone looks at you rather than looking down at your phone or making a mean face. We children of God need to be approachable so when people see our light, they realize it's a loving sun that offers comfort and hope.
- Practice talking to strangers at the grocery store, mall, etc. If you're trying out a new product and see someone doing the same, ask questions and then remember to listen! Ease yourself into sharing things about yourself during the conversation. You might meet someone who's been overseas, and that could be a good time to mention your travel dreams.
- Practice your listening skills with friends, family, and strangers by letting them do most of the talking.

Prayer

Lord, I pray that you help us accept that we are the salt of the earth who bring unique seasonings to this world, which brings you glory. Give us boldness and help us better interact with people so we might reach some. Help us be open vessels to be used as you will anytime and anyhow no matter how uncomfortable the situation. Lord, teach us we are enough and don't have to prove it to anyone.

CHAPTER 3

It's Contagious

I thought I was walking into a regular Wednesday night Bible study, but right as I stepped into the sanctuary, I knew something was different. My pastor announced he was going to hand the microphone to the church's youth leader, who gave a testimony about the youth retreat they had been on the previous weekend.

He testified about how eighteen young people became filled with the Holy Spirit and ten were refilled. He said that when they got back to church, three more were filled. He explained how on fire these youths were when they experienced the glory of God; they had spoken in tongues. They were determined to bask in His presence, and they prayed for five hours after they got back. Some parents were confused at what they saw, but these bold kids laid hands on their parents so they could have a taste of the glory of God as well. They laid hands on each other and prayed over themselves and their families.

My heart was full, especially when they mentioned that some five- and seven-year-olds had also received the Holy Spirit and had spoken in tongues. It was so beautiful, but that was just a snippet of what God had in store for us that night.

The youth couldn't stay in their seats; they were moving toward the stage in prayer, just itching for more of God's glory. My pastor said he would flow with the Spirit and let them pray. The youth ran toward the congregation, praying and laying hands. They spoke boldly in tongues and prophesied all over the building. This amazing sight brought the whole congregation to tears.

When the adults started worshipping God and speaking in tongues, I realized that when God allows His glory to shine through us, it can cause a ripple effect. His glory is contagious. The number of youths there was less than the number of adults, but we could feel their passion for God, and it stirred our hearts and awoke in us a love and thirst for God like never before! We all left that service with full hearts.

God reminded me of when I first spoke in tongues on Pentecost Sunday in 2012. I grew up knowing about the Holy Spirit and speaking in tongues, but I thought it was just something older people did. I didn't think I had to worry about it till I was at least thirty. But during my second year in college, I learned my roommate could speak in tongues. I was curious. *Lord, I thought it was just for old people. Maybe she's the exception to the rule,* I thought.

As the Lord would have it, I started attending a new Bible study and began to learn more about the Holy Spirit. I found out my theory about old people was incorrect. A certain desire began to stir in me when I realized the gift was accessible to me. One day, I came into Bible study and heard the Lord whisper, "When you get baptized, you will receive the Holy Spirit."

My parents baptized me when I was too young to understand it, so I was excited to be baptized again, this time having made a conscious choice. I hunted down every baptism service I could find, but it never worked out. On Pentecost Sunday at my church, as God would have it, there was a spontaneous baptism that took place, and I felt the Lord say, "Go!" Yeah! My hair wasn't done, I wasn't prepared, and I didn't plan to be baptized, but it was God's timing, so I went with it.

We often fall prey to our definition of what being "prepared" means and forget we are to live according to God's standards, not ours. His ways and thoughts are above ours, so we must rest in His instructions even when they go against everything we've planned.

The church gave us clothes to change into, and before I got to the baptismal pool, I was bawling my eyes out because God's presence was so thick in church. The Lord was working on my heart and breaking down my walls. As I was dunked into the water, I almost instantly felt restored. I changed out of my wet clothes and went back to my seat. The pastor said that if anyone felt a tug to get the Holy Spirit, he or she should come up front. Usually, my first thought would have been, *Err, uh, I'm not about to stand in front of the church looking ashy-bodied. I'll go if I get some lotion.* But I felt a great desire for the Holy Spirit; I wanted the Holy Spirit more than my pride in my appearance and others' approval.

That day, I hit my all-time record of "How much can you cry in one day" because I knew I didn't deserve it and wasn't sure why I wanted it. But I couldn't deny my thirst. I stood at the altar for a time. It seemed that everyone around me was receiving the Holy Spirit except me. I didn't understand why. I thought, *Maybe today isn't the day after all. I'll just head to me seat.* I stood up. The Lord stopped me. He told me to fight for Him, to push past how I was feeling, and hang in there because that was the day He had destined for me to be filled. So I stayed. After some minutes, He pointed out an elder and said, "When she comes to pray with you, you will speak in tongues."

A couples minutes later, she came over to me, and just as he said, I started speaking in tongues. God's glory fell so heavy on me that I fell to my knees in awe of how mighty He was. I tried to stop speaking just to say thank you, but I couldn't. What I felt coming out of my mouth was like a rushing wave of heavenly melodies that had been waiting to come out.

When I finally caught my breath, I smiled and raised my hands and worshipped God. I stood up like a warrior who had just won a battle. I wondered if that was how David felt when he killed Goliath. The reason I hadn't spoken in tongues before that was that my heart hadn't been ready for the seed to be planted. Our hearts represent the soil in which heavenly seeds are planted, but planting doesn't ensure proper growth. My timing had been off, and I'm glad it had been, because when I received the gift of speaking in tongues, I knew God had given it to me; it had nothing to do with my ability but everything to do with His plan.

Don't let the Enemy convince you that when you don't get what you want, God must have changed His mind. Isaiah 56 tells us that every word God has spoken will not return to Him void but will accomplish everything He has said. Wait on the Lord. What might look like delay is really just divine orchestration.

I felt so much peace and joy that day, and seeing those kids basking in that same glory just set a fire in my soul. I thought, *What if we take this fire and passion stirred up within us and pour it out to the world?*

It seems that God does things for us but that we share them only with people in our inner circles, those we feel comfortable with. These kids, however, were bold just like our Father and refused to be limited to cliques. They simply found the nearest person and poured out the love of God. That may sound scary, but look at it this way: someone's breakthrough is dependent on our obedience. What if others were disobedient when God sent them to us? Maybe we wouldn't have received certain words from God.

Myles Monroe once said he wanted to leave this world empty; he wanted to pour out everything God put in him— gifts, glories, seeds—and share it with the world. That should be our mind-set. Until we can come to Christ like children and be willing to follow Him whether we understand where we are going or not, we will never fulfill our purpose.

Our little spark can set everyone we come in contact with on fire, but shielded flames don't spread. Imagine if we made ourselves always available to God to share a piece of that unending passion in us. Our purpose is to go into the world and be lights not for ourselves but for others. The beginning of this journey starts with obedience.

Practical Tips

- It can be scary to approach people even when we know God has given us a message, so we need to get our flesh to back off. Sometimes, the fear of rejection scares us away. It helps me when I give myself a pep talk and command my flesh to be silent. We should tell ourselves, "There is nothing a human can do to me that can diminish the Word of God. They cannot do anything to me that God does not allow. His words are all that matter, and if I'm rejected, I'll hold on to the fact Jesus was also rejected. As long as I'm in His will and obey, He'll take care of the rest."

- If you aren't comfortable with big groups, start with smaller groups. Join godly ministries that encourage intimate fellowships and share your testimony there. This helps to get you used to talking in front of crowds.

- Write down your testimony and key lessons you learned so you have main points when speaking. Of course, if the Spirit takes over, the list doesn't matter.

- Those of us who can speak in tongues should not let that blessing lie dormant. The Enemy hears our prayers and can counteract us by reminding us of our inefficiency. By praying in this language the Enemy will never understand, we get an upper hand when communing with the Lord.

- If you've been trying to receive the gift of speaking in tongues, don't give up. You are a step closer than you were yesterday. Don't be limited to your church;

commune with God in your personal prayer closet. I have heard testimonies of people getting filled in their bedrooms, and God can do the same for you.

Prayer

Lord, please give us the opportunity to share the passion and fire you have put in us. Help us to be brave enough to share our testimonies when you provide platforms for us to reveal what you have done on our behalf. For those out there without your Holy Spirit, Lord, ignite a hunger for more of you and show yourself to them in a magnificent way.

CHAPTER 4

Career Path

Most of my life, I knew I wanted to be a writer, but I wasn't sure what I wanted to write or how I would write it. I can fall in love with a new hobby but then drop it two minutes later. I then move on to the next one. That was a reason I'd been confused. I walked with my head up as if I knew my left from my right, faking the walk of one who had it all together, but I was actually just as confused as the next person.

I wanted to believe I had a plan for my life. I couldn't tell what God's plan was for my life, and I was too impatient to wait for Him to reveal it, so I made up a fairytale future. Faith is the evidence of things not seen but hoped for (Hebrews 11:1). I had no faith in God because I wanted something and He wasn't giving it to me; I wanted to hear Him, but He wasn't speaking to me when I wanted to hear it. So I took control of my future.

I made up a lie and dwelled on it for so long it that it became my reality. Things went downhill from there. I began to eat, breathe, sleep, and live according to that lie, but thank God for grace.

I made the mistake of starting college as a science major. I thought if I wasn't studying sciences or engineering, why bother going to school, right? Wrong! Before I went to college, the Lord encouraged me to look into a different field, but I didn't listen because I wanted to earn good money. I'd see everyone in my field of study flourishing, but I was miserable. I would study hard, and it seemed I could even teach others, but I was getting the lowest grades. I'd cry till I ran out of tears; I was frustrated. My made-up future of becoming a pharmacist and paying off my loans, taking care of my family, and paying my bills wasn't looking feasible.

One of the requirements for my major was calculus, but math and I aren't friends. I studied very hard for one particular exam; I even attended tutoring sessions. I was feeling confident on the day of the exam; I walked into the exam hall thinking I was going to kill it. After the exam, I imagined my A+, but later that night, I learned I had earned a D, not even a D+, which would have allowed me to say that at least that + in my proclamation had been right.

It felt like my heart had been hit so many times; I was about to give up. I had so much going on, and my mind was all over the place. But what did I expect when I was trying to handle a job that was meant for God? I went home, and as soon as I shut my door, tears rolled down my face. I fell to the ground and cried out to God. Nothing seemed to be going right. I thought God had left me. *Father, is this punishment?* I asked Him.

My roommate found me in a state of depression. I tried to explain to her with tears in my eyes how my heart had taken enough blows to last a lifetime. Her phone rang, and on the other end was a word straight from heaven.

One song has a line, "He's an on time God, yes He is on time," and I've always been familiar with it, but on that day, it was in sync with my spirit. My roommate's mother said the Lord laid it on her heart to tell me it was going to be all right and I shouldn't give up. It might not have been a whole sermon, but it saved me from something unknown. Who knows what would have happened if that word hadn't come to me? I could have gone out to seek comfort from a god that I felt would have been of immediate help.

Choosing a Major

After a while, I began to feel a tug on my heart to switch my major from biology to marketing. I'm sure some of you, especially Africans out there, can relate to my mental struggle. *Oh, so you don't mind starving after graduation? You want to soak garri for the rest of your life then?* That was the response I imagined I would get from my family. By the way, garri is a West African food made from dried cassava tubers; when you're broke, it's pretty much the most affordable food you'll find.

The basic mentality in some African countries is that only certain majors are worth studying, and business and marketing were not among them. I engaged in the wrestling Jacob had engaged in—it was that intense. I had spent almost six years as a science major, so how could I switch to a totally different field? *Lord, why would you have me waste all this time and now ask me to move?*

But the truth was that I had felt that tug the whole six years I was studying science. I was just never able to gather the courage to move on until I hit that wall, the one that stops you dead in your tracks and makes you stare at your decision in the face. You're cornered, and you have to choose. In that case, I had two choices. Either I picked God's best for me even though I had no clue how He would get me there, or I stuck to the misery I knew.

The answer seems obvious. Who in his or her right mind would pick misery over God? As crazy as it sounds, I did. As a matter of fact, I chose misery for so many years because I was familiar with it. I knew what to expect on my path, and I knew I had no control over the other. The idea of not being in control made me afraid.

Every day, I would learn things that never excited me; I never saw myself living the rest of my life that way, but I settled for fear. I gave it more reverence than I was giving God. I see a generation that would rather settle for what others think or see than trust God. I've been in that space before and can relate.

However, after God delivered me, I saw that His plans could not be compared to what we could see. I know how tormenting the feeling of uncertainty can be, but being in control of our destinies will have us going around in circles. It hurts less when we surrender to His plan.

Eventually, I realized God wanted more for me, and I asked Him to show up in my situation. I applied to the college of business and left it at that. Shortly after, I was accepted.

The transition wasn't easy, but the difference was that I put God in control. I started walking the path that ensured an expected end. Just knowing He was in control eased my mind. For the first time in a while, I experienced an indescribable peace.

God wants to give this same peace to everyone going down a path He didn't ordain for them. It may seem like picking a major is just a little thing, but God cares so much about even the smallest facets of our lives.

> How precious to me are your thoughts, God! How vast is the sum of them!
> Were I to count them, they would outnumber the grains of sand when I awake I am still with you. (Psalm 139:17–18 NIV)

His thoughts outnumber the grains of sand. Imagine trying to count the grains in just a handful of sand. But we serve a God whose thoughts surpass the grains of sand on the earth, and all those thoughts are good! That's a lot of thoughts. So the next time the Enemy tries to tell you God doesn't care about an area of your life, remind him about God's word through David. God cares. You are always on His mind.

The Search Begins

I refused to be uncertain about life after college. I put on my big-girl pants and hustled for a big-girl job. I searched high and low and filled out innumerable applications. I'd had many jobs; I'd been a coffee maker, hair stylist, a turn assistant (a fancy term for a painter/furniture mover/cleaner), call-center representative, door-to-door salesperson, gas station attendant—the list goes on. I'd never been without a job during the times I wasn't in school, and I wanted a meaningful job after graduation.

I had one interview after another, and I received one rejection after another. I began to think all my extracurricular activities, leadership roles, and experiences weren't going to pay off. Disney magic really wasn't so magical after all.

Then I got word a big company wanted to interview me over the phone. When I read that email, I was ecstatic. My phone interview led to a whole-day interview, but I had to wait almost two months to find out if I would get the job.

During that time, my mind was racing. I wanted the job badly. I prayed, pled, and bugged God to tell them to hurry up. I had felt good after the interview, and I knew deep down I was going to get it, but that didn't curb my impatience.

God has given us a promise, and God doesn't lie; His Word will not return to Him void, yet we still fall into doubt when we can't see His promise becoming real. That waiting tested my patience. I wasn't applying for any other jobs maybe because I had exhausted all my resources and I had a tingle in my spirit that kept reassuring me of this job. So I waited.

One morning, I got a call. The company made an offer; I was ecstatic! Everything was looking amazing. I guess the Disney magic finally caught up; I joke, I joke. I know Jesus had come through.

New Beginning?

I started the job shortly after graduation, and I had to train for about three months. Almost right away, I knew something was off about the place. I felt so different from almost everyone I met but didn't understand why. The conversations, the beliefs, what people did for fun, the interactions I had with others—everything seemed off, but I tried to brush that off. I thought God had given me the job, so it was going to work out somehow.

During that time, I experienced some of the hardest months of my life. I was constantly on the move, traveling from city to city, state to state, hotel to hotel. I love traveling, new experiences, but something was missing.

Soon enough, I realized this part of corporate America was going to be rough. To excel, I felt I had to fit in and become someone I wasn't. I had been in situations like that numerous times. Whenever I'd had to change myself to please people, I always ended up by myself, alone and empty.

After God revealed that I didn't need to please everyone, I prayed He would help me not be so easily swayed, and He did. My state of mind during that season can best be described in this verse: "My heart is fixed O Lord" (Psalm 57:7 NIV).

In that case, my heart was immovably set on the standard God had laid out for me. I was convinced all the lessons God had taught me over the years were for a reason. No amount of money, no title, no human being, nothing could move me except God. I refused to lower my standards or shush the Holy Spirit to appease man. I learned a great deal about myself through that process.

During my training, I had to complete a project and present it to management. I was given resources, and I was determined to excel. I went over and above to show my managers I was capable and prove that even if I wasn't into the same things they were, I would be able to perform my job flawlessly.

On presentation day, I was nervous even after having practiced my presentation. I had practiced so much my brain must have been sick of me. I probably recited my presentation in my sleep. Before I went in, I prayed for favor. I saw God's hand move as He eased my nervous mind and assured me I didn't need to fear anyone or prove myself because He had already done that on the cross for me.

After my presentation, I was given feedback on my ability to answer questions, present findings, and so on. I knew I surely hadn't had all the answers to the questions I'd been asked, but I put in the effort to present the necessary data. One of my supervisors commended me on such a great presentation flow and my ability to command the attention of my audience. I had a praise break just in my head; it would have been unprofessional to get on the floor and praise God right then. My praise break was short lived, however. I received a very disgruntled comment.

Another manager told me, "This was a very disappointing presentation to say the least. You met no expectations whatsoever, and there were a lot of holes. Usually, we give people a grade, but in this case, you're upgradable."

I choose to believe my mouth didn't drop to the floor in shock. I remember thinking, *What in the world is happening?* After a discussion, I drove back to my hotel. I didn't know what to do, so I ended up doing what I usually do after things happen that I don't understand. I usually analyzed the situation, but in this case, I analyzed the words he had spoken. Dwelling on negative words can harm a person's mind. It's no wonder Philippians 4:8 KJV tells us,

> Finally, brethren, whatsoever things are true, whatsoever things are honest, whatsoever things are just, whatsoever things are pure, whatsoever things are lovely, whatsoever things are of good report; if there be any virtue, and if there be any praise, think on these things.

His words raised doubts in my mind. I thought, *How is it possible a college graduate cannot deliver a presentation? How am I supposed to be effective in the kingdom when I'm over here disappointing people? I'm so bad I can't even fit on a grading scale?* But overanalyzing things has never led to a good ending; I should have known better than to dwell on those words. I doubted myself, and what made me mad was that someone would tell me I hadn't done a good job when I thought I had. Were his words on the harsh side? Yes, but the Lord checked my pride in this situation; He showed me I wasn't above making mistakes. I decided to retrace my steps and make sure I had the knowledge I needed to be the best I could be. I talked to my managers to understand in detail what I could have done better, and I sent an updated presentation to all of them.

On September 11, 2014, I was fired. I felt so free after typing that, because some people still don't even know what happened for many reasons. One reason is that I felt shamed and as if I had let people down. Who gets fired from training and can't really explain why?

> And of this gospel I was appointed a herald and an apostle and a teacher. That is why I am suffering as I am. Yet this is no cause for shame, because I know whom I have believed, and am convinced that he is able to guard what I have entrusted to him until that day. (2 Timothy 1:11–12 NIV)

Paul reminds us in this chapter not to be ashamed of the path God has us walking. We often let the Devil blind us with humiliation, and that causes us to forget that everything works out for the good of those who love God.

Your today is temporary, and when you face tribulations, don't hide; rather, praise God for the victory that is to come. On the day I was fired, those same words that had started a war in my spirit were used on me once again by the same manager. I almost stood up at the meeting and rebuked him. But you know how corporate America can be when you decide to express yourself. So I rebuked him gently in my head.

However, God had warned me about what was going to happen that day, so I hadn't been caught off guard, but that didn't stop my spirit from wrestling with those words.

It hurt me more than I can explain. The thought that this man had assumed it was okay to say what he had to another human with such superiority in his tone and without a valid reason shocked me.

But remember how I said before that God was always on time? Well, He showed up once again. He'll never fail to show up right when you need Him the most. He reminded me of a billboard I read the day before on my way home: "Absolutely Beyond Expectation."

The situation didn't make sense, but one thing I knew was that God is intentional. Look at the story of Joseph and his brothers in the Bible. We may say his brothers were wicked for selling him into slavery because they were jealous of the love their father had for him. The reason for their action was definitely bad, but God had a bigger plan. Think about it: if Joseph had never been sold, he would have never been able to interpret Pharaoh's dream, which earned him an esteemed position. When there was shortage of food back in Joseph's hometown, his father sent his brothers to Egypt for food. Joseph ultimately revealed his identity to his brothers and didn't hold their actions against them because it had all been in God's plan.

> "Come closer to me," Joseph said to his brothers. They came closer. "I am Joseph your brother whom you sold into Egypt. But don't feel badly, don't blame yourselves for selling me. God was behind it. God sent me here ahead of you to save lives. There has been a famine in the land now for two years; the famine will continue for five more

years-neither plowing nor harvesting. God sent
me on ahead to pave the way and make sure there
was a remnant in the land, to save your lives in an
amazing act of deliverance. So you see, it wasn't
you who sent me here but God. He set me in place
as a father to Pharaoh, put me in charge of his
personal affairs, and made me ruler of all Egypt."
(Genesis 45:4–8 Message)

This story depicts God's intentional nature. Nothing
happens without His approval, and He knows the end from
the beginning. What may seem strange to us may just be
God orchestrating a solution to a future problem.

I was actually pretty calm after getting fired. Later on, I
did cry, but what hurt me the most was that someone let me
go rather than giving me an option to leave. The Lord was
definitely working on that pride factor during that process.
After discussing the whole situation with one of my teachers,
she urged me to find lessons in my experience. I did.

Lesson One

As children of God, we have to guard our hearts from the
words we take in and dwell on. We can't just let anyone
speak negative words over our lives, and even if they do, we
must reaffirm ourselves with the Word of God and believe
what He says about us rather than what anyone else says
about us. People, in this case corporate America, try to fit

us into this human-calculated capability scale that in reality just limits our ability to expand.

Whatever you do, don't let the words or "grades" given by mere people weigh you down or cause you to think less of yourself. Whose "grading" of you have you been accepting?

There is no way you can accept both God's and people's view of you. Actually, it was good I couldn't fit into the human-calculated scale because it showed me I was set apart. Children of God are set apart for a higher purpose; they have been called to achieve way more than humanity can imagine.

I'm not suggesting to those in corporate America to quit their jobs; they should just keep in mind that when this world passes away, only God's grading of us will stand. It's what He says about us that matters. Not to say He cannot use our bosses to speak to us, but we must be careful to assess whether it is the voice of truth. If the words don't line up with the Word or there isn't a godly conviction, it's not God.

> The grass withers and the flowers fall, but the word of our God endures forever. (Isaiah 40:8 NIV)

His grading of us is "absolutely beyond expectation" not because we are good in ourselves but as a result of the price Jesus paid for us. When God looks at us, He sees the precious blood Jesus shed to save the world. Since we are made in the image and likeness of God and He is the epitome of excellence, we cannot be anything short of that. We sure aren't God, but since we are a reflection of Him, we have that excellent spirit in us as well.

Lesson Two

I am not above mistakes, and all children of God should be humble. If we aren't able to take correction, how can God show us those things that don't please Him and mold us into whom we are meant to become?

After all my complaining about how I didn't understand why they thought my presentation was unsatisfactory, the Lord cautioned me about my pride and told me something that hurt but that was for my own good. He explained how I had been so caught up my version of the story that I ignored all the corrections they gave me.

Whether I thought it was incorrect or not, there wasn't anything wrong with me going over my work and looking through the corrections. A proud heart says, "I know everything, and my way is the best way," but a humble heart is aware of its flaws and is open to criticism because it understands the result is growth.

That's not to say we should take the word of all our critics at face value. However, if our bosses or managers correct our work, we should look into those corrections and determine if we had indeed omitted something.

> The pride of your heart had deceived you, you who
> live in the clefts of the rocks and make your home

on the heights, you who say to yourself, 'who can bring me down? (Obadiah 1:3 NIV)

We can become so self-absorbed that all we can see is what we want to see, but God will bring us to reality. He helped me see I had been blinded by the façade of perfection that caused me to ignore not only the corrections at work but also His corrections. Just like a leopard cannot hide it spots, we cannot be one way with people and another way with God. Who we are with people is a direct reflection of who we are in Christ. We can't claim to treat God better than we treat His people. When we choose our ways over God's, what we're saying is that we know better than He does. But no student is greater than his or her teacher (John 13:16), and our knowledge can never exceed His.

Lesson Three

Material things can lead to happiness, but they can never produce eternal joy. For a while, I prayed God would restore my joy; I knew that providing just for myself wasn't enough. The happiness I felt when I looked at my bank account was always short lived; it was overshadowed by the echoes in my heart that longed to be filled with His joy.

God has created you for more than just passing through life with temporal happiness. Sure, you want to pay your bills and take care of others, but if you've ever experienced joy, you'll understand it can't be traded for anything in this world. Monetary needs can always be met by God, but chasing money will divert us from chasing God.

> No one can serve two masters; for either he will hate the one and love the other, or else he will be loyal to the one and despise the other. You cannot serve God and mammon. (Matthew 6:24 NKJV)

If you're on a particular career or path because you want to make money, you're not serving God. Work can take a majority of your time, and granted, you may not be called to a travel the world and preach the gospel, but God has set aside a field for you to labor in. He has called some people into the corporate environment to represent Him. When you are chasing money, the last thing on your minds is using your job as a platform to honor God.

Lesson Four

We must trust God even when our vision seems blurry. We must continue to rest on the dreams He has revealed to us. I learned that when God is taking us somewhere, most times, only He and we understand where that is. All we can do is follow His lead to His expected end for us. Even the people closest to us may not quite get it; they might even have plans of their own for how our lives should be, but God's plan is perfect.

You may not be able to see past where you are now, but know that God has the master plan. The vision He gave you is for just you, and sometimes, it means you'll have to walk through seasons hand in hand with God. But that should be great news, as He can take you places you could only dream about. In Him, you've got everything you will ever need. Even when you have lost something, just hold on to His promise. Don't let the Enemy cause doubt in your mind and lead you into mourning over your loss; rather, rejoice that if you lost it, then greater things are on the way.

There is a huge difference between living and surviving. One is God's plan, and the other is humanity's plan. Jesus said He came so we would have life and have it more abundantly (John 10:10). When we settle for our plan, we sacrifice the life He died for in exchange for barely making it.

No matter how great a person's life appears, if it's a life without Jesus, it's an empty life. To live life in abundance, we have to seek the one in whom abundance dwells. And an abundant life means so much more than money; it includes peace of mind, joy, rest, and many other great gifts God has for those who love Him.

I believe that God let me lose my job because I probably wouldn't have ever had the courage to quit and pursue my passion. As much as I wished I had voluntarily left, I know deep down I wouldn't have because it would have meant I'd be back in the pool of uncertainty. The dysfunction I knew was slowly becoming my cocaine, and if He didn't cut off that supply, I probably would have died from an overdose of pure depression.

God, however, loves us so much that He refuses to let us stay in our holes and be miserable. We may not think we are in the best situations, but God is saving us from lives of regret. He is ordering our footsteps to lead us to the glorious end He planned when He called us all by name.

Practical Tips

- If you're looking into a particular field to major in or build a career, write down your passions and aspirations first so you can develop a clear picture for yourself of what you want.
- Consult God before entering any field of study. Pray, fast, read your Word, and listen to Him for His plan. Ask Him for confirmation after doing these things and watch Him work.
- Do not major in an area because of money. God gives the provision, not your job, so rest on Him and follow the passion He has given you.
- If you're already in a major but can't decide if it's right for you, make a list of what you have a passion for on one side, and on the other side, list your reasons for studying your major. Compare your lists and talk to God about it.
- If you're already working and are feeling God tugging on your heart to leave your job, be obedient. It may mean you won't have another job for a while and will just sit still in His presence. It may mean you have to dust off your resume and look for another job, but it will be worth it. Every moment you stay in a job that's not for you, the stronger its hold on you will become, and it will hurt to invest so much in something that

wasn't yours to begin with. There is fruit waiting for you to harvest on the other side, where God's promise is waiting for you. Trust that when He shows you your field, your gift will make room for you.

- God gives the provision, not humanity, so your paycheck is by God's grace, not your company's. God has no expiration date, but mammon—money and everything contrary to God—does. Will you choose to settle for something you know won't last or the One who is eternal?

Prayer

Lord, teach us to be obedient to you even when it means going against popular views. Help us seek your will above ours, and give us strength to walk on the narrow path you have called us to. Father, we pray for faith in your direction and strength to move past our feelings and walk the path you set for us. Give us a humble spirit that receives conviction from you and applies it to our lives.

CHAPTER 5

Runaway Bride

It has taken me so long to admit this. It has taken heartache, tears, depression, and getting my love thrown back in my face to figure out that true commitment scares me. My mind can be quite complicated. Yeah, I said I wanted commitment, but in the same breath, I didn't believe it was possible for me to commit myself. That phobia of mine was affecting my relationship with God. The issue was just a branch of a much bigger problem I had; I didn't have the hope that stems from the seed of true love.

Our lives should be reflections of Jesus. He is love, and when we say He dwells in us, our reflection should be identical to love. How do we know what love looks like? We must understand God is love in its essence. To learn what love is, we need to spend time with Him and let Him show us every layer that makes Him who He is. Here is an excerpt from one of my blog posts titled, "Marriage: For Better or Worse."

Relationships don't work out most of the time because people have no tolerance for our worst, and

41

I'm sure we can think about some characteristic we have that could push people away. We even cheat on God sometimes, but I'm thankful that when He said He was in it for better or worse, He meant it.

There is only so much the human vessel will agree to take, but God is in it for the good, the bad, and the ugly. But you know why people in relationships can tolerate another person only to an extent? It's because they haven't gasped what a real relationship is about. How can anyone love another for better or worse if he or she doesn't understand Jesus Christ?

Jesus is love, and until you are thoroughly committed to your relationship with Him, other relationships, including marriages, won't work out.

You might say, "I don't have anyone I am in a relationship with," but I'm not just talking about significant others; this is also relevant in friendships as well. Having friends means being married to them in a sense; they shouldn't leave you when you need them the most, right? You share your life and emotions with them, right? When your best friend gets another best friend and forgets about you, that hurts, right? That certainly hurts me, and that's why I equate friendships and marriage.

Until I learned to see others with the eyes of God, my relationships just didn't work. For us to be able to have a real relationship with another person, we have to first have a working marriage with God. We are taught to love our neighbors with the love of God, but how can we love them if we don't know what that love looks like? Since God is love, we have to spend time with Him to understand how love behaves, endures, rejoices, and tolerates.

Most of my relationships didn't work out because their foundations were wrong from the start. If love—Jesus—was the rock on which we built our relationships, they would endure. If those foundations were laid on our desires, our focus would be selfish.

Time removes the weeds pretending to be real plants. No matter how connected those weeds of ungodly relationships were to your branches or how painful their removal was, for you to flourish, something had to die. Maybe you haven't reached the stage where those weeds have been cut off and are finding it hard to let go even when you've felt God tug on your heart about certain relationships.

Trust God and let go because weeds suck out life and potential from you. Weeds stunt your growth, and hanging on to them could cause you to be cut off. In John 15, Jesus spoke about the branches and the vine. He explained how every unfruitful branch would be cut off and every fruitful branch pruned to produce more fruit. Which branch will you choose to be today?

The pruning of the unwanted parts leads to fruitfulness, but the attachment to them leads to death. Please, choose to live today.

Longing to be Filled

I have never embraced the beauty of being alone; loneliness scared me more than almost anything else. I remember walking through the snow to the bus stop from school one day when I lived in England. I poured out my heart to God as I cried. My heart felt so sad and abandoned. *Will this ever end, Lord*? It seemed that I would spend eternity by myself.

I didn't have any friends; I had just moved from Nigeria, and I wasn't having any luck making friends at school. Maybe I was just awkward or a little freaked out when one girl ran her hands through my braids and said, "I just had to feel it! I've never seen anything like this before," and she kept staring at me!

Usually, having at least something in common with someone else would help, but I was the only black female in my school, and that made it harder for me. I felt very alone no matter how hard I tried to fit in.

Then I moved to America, made some friends, and *bam!* I was finally smiling again. I had graduated from high school in Nigeria when I was fifteen, and in America, I found out I was very young to be in college. To make an easier adjustment, I repeated my final year of high school before heading to college.

Surprisingly, that wasn't a bad transition, and toward the end, the Lord began to speak to me about how He was getting ready to steal me to Himself. He wanted me to be alone with Him.

Then I graduated college and moved to a city where I had no family or friends. I ate dinner most times by myself, and during one of those days, I got over my phobia of going to the movies alone. It used to be creepy, but God drew my attention to the fact that although I may not have seen Him, He had always been and would always be with me. That day, when I cried in the snow, He was there catching every single one of my tears.

> You keep track of all my sorrows. You have collected all my tears in your bottle. You have recorded each one in your book. (Psalm 56:8 NLT)

He was holding me so close and felt my pain. He understood what I was going through because He had been in a similar situation. He was in love with a sinner who loved the world more than she loved Him. She wouldn't even spend time with Him unless she had a request. She claimed Him only when it was convenient. It was much like the story of the unfaithful wife who chose adultery over her husband in the book of Hosea. It wasn't that he didn't love her enough, because he did, more than words could describe. He married her despite her reputation, her past, her sins, herself. Though she cheated on him in her search for valuables, not knowing what she already had couldn't be bought or even earned, He still pursued her. This love story between Jesus and His adulterous church signifies the relationship between Jesus and us.

I felt an empty space in my heart that longed for companionship; it longed to be filled. The Lord showed me I was feeling the same pain He felt every day I put another human being or thing above Him. Every time, I removed Him from the throne of my heart, put Him to the side, and replaced Him with an idol. I ran away from Him thinking other people could fill my void, but the missing piece to my puzzle had been standing right in front of me the whole time.

God is jealous for you. You have been created to give God a unique glory, and every day you give that glory to something else, you rob God.

I Want the Whole Package

Have you ever had a song get stuck in your head? For a while, I had "All of Me," a song by John Legend, stuck in my head. When I first heard the song, I imagined what it would be like to meet my Adam. It painted a picture of a love story I hoped my name would be a part of someday. Too engrossed in this fairytale, I didn't realize I was already involved in a love story soon to be unveiled for the world to see.

A perfect God was glancing down on an imperfect woman, and instead of seeing her as the world and as she saw herself, He saw perfection. Every spot on her was precious to Him. He wanted her, and He wanted everything she came with—not only her beauty but also her every blemish, flaw, and shortcoming. He loved all of her.

Even though the song is cute, no one can love without God. Any love shown is really an extension of God's love given freely to them.

> Love is patient, love is kind. It does not envy, it does not boast, it is not proud. It does not dishonor

others, it is not self-seeking, it is not easily angered, it keeps no record of wrongs. Love does not delight in evil but rejoices with truth. It always protects, always trusts, always hopes, always perseveres. Love never fails. (1 Corinthians 13:4–8a NIV)

This Scripture paints a picture of love in its purest form. It's one thing to talk about the love of God, but it's another to recognize we are to be a witness of His everlasting love. In 1 John 2:6, we read that whoever claims to live in Him must live as Jesus did. As human beings, we more often than not love conditionally, most of the time just when it's convenient for us. We love the parts of people we agree with or that align with our values and morals. I'm not saying we should love others' sin; we must love the sinner and despise the sin. That's not easy to do due to our human nature, but it isn't impossible.

One day, God told me, "You have to spend time with love to know how to love." God is love, so it's no wonder there are so many bad relationships and not many lasting marriages. We missed the foundation of it all. We have settled for a mediocre imitation of what love is, and we wonder why our love seems to fade so soon. God is everlasting, so to learn how to love without boundaries, we have to know him first.

The Seed of Loneliness

It's been one long roller-coaster, I tell you, when it comes to relationships with significant others. I have never been a girl who ended up with the guy she liked or was "chosen" by a guy. In my case, there always seemed to be another person in the picture. I remember the first person I dated way back. For a moment, it all seemed to be going well, but then one thing led to another, and she came along.

Unfortunately, that was the trend in most of my previous relationships. I guessed that when they figured out I was serious about not losing my pride until marriage, they decided to get it elsewhere. I liked each person I dated, but I just couldn't open up to them in that way. I've made so many mistakes in my life, but that was one value I upheld because I don't believe I'd be able to face God if I didn't.

Although generalizations aren't always accurate, I felt they wanted just sex, and since I wasn't letting the cookie out of the jar, they went to a different pot. The frequency of this situation was abnormal, so I decided to take an inventory. I concluded that either there was something wrong with me or that all guys were the same. Of course, no one likes to admit there is something wrong with himself or herself, so I went for option B—all guys are the same. That didn't mean I wouldn't try to get to know people, but it limited my ability to open up to them. I walked into relationships with a firm belief that all men wanted was sex.

I had been hurt so many times that I built up psychological defenses. When my relationships got to the point that people were getting into territories in my heart I had labeled off limits, I shut down. My thinking was that I didn't have to let someone into my heart who was going to be just like the rest.

As much as we want to believe we aren't biased and we try to objectively analyze situations, sometimes, that isn't the case. We're most likely to accept whatever "truth" is easier to handle. That's exactly what I did. Rather than trying to figure out what I was doing to contribute to this vicious cycle, I shut out guys. If I didn't let them into the deepest parts of my heart, it would be easier to let them go if it didn't work. I was wrong because I labeled people without giving them a chance. And the mechanism wasn't as bulletproof as I thought; my heart still hurt.

Why did I even care so much? I begged God to please take the heart He had given me that made me feel too much for people who never seemed to think about me. I remember countless times when I soaked my pillow in tears, hoping God would see how much pain my heart caused me. Was this supposed to be a gift or a life sentence of bondage?

When I was done with my pity party, God revealed to me the truth about why those relationships hadn't worked out. I was as much to blame as any of the guys. I was attracting what my heart was reflecting—things of the flesh, not things of the spirit. Even if the people with the spirit of God, whom I claimed I was trying to attract, saw me, they wouldn't recognize me because the fruits I bore were of my flesh.

No doubt I was saved, Holy Spirit filled, tongue speaking, demon casting, and Bible reading, but my heart hadn't been totally transformed into the heart of God, especially concerning this area. I still had junk and ideologies that had built up in me over the years. I was chasing physical characteristics; I was too in love with the potential of whom they could turn out to be. I thought that even though they weren't so great at the present, their futures looked bright, so that was okay with me. Someone once said, "Never fall in love with someone's potential, because if he or she doesn't realize it, you'll be the one disappointed."

We often fall in love with whom we think someone will become, and we miss who he or she presently is. After getting into a relationship, the veil that clouded our vision is torn open. We become discontent when we don't see changes in the person overnight. There's nothing wrong in seeing potential in people, but not loving them in their present, flaws and all, sets us up for heartbreak. We should not fall so in love with their futures that we forget to love their "present."

I had this list of qualities I wanted in a significant other, but most were physical and very superficial. Soon enough, I realized those qualities could never replace a person who truly had the heart of God in him. Yeah, I said I wanted a man who loved Jesus more than he loved me, but deep down, I just wanted someone so I wouldn't be alone. I said I wanted someone who loved unconditionally, was patient, enduring, trustworthy, honest, prayerful, and wise. I wanted a "perfect" man, but he doesn't exist. I learned that it wasn't so much about what characteristics I wanted as much as who I was.

Ask yourself if you possess the characteristics your significant other wants.

> Thus, by their fruit you will recognize them.
> (Matthew 7:20 NIV)

God has set aside your significant other, bone of your bone, flesh of your flesh, but there are processes you must go through to be ready to receive this gift from God. There are certain fruits you pray for in your significant other, and chances are they're praying for the same fruits in you. Even if you were in the same room, he or she might not be able to recognize you, because your fruits don't match what God has promised him or her. You can spend so much time making up your lists that you forget to prepare yourself for the gift.

After all the tears, I shut down completely. I wasn't up for any more heartache. What happened was that during this "strike," I also shut the Lord out. Deep down, I felt a void, and I thought it was the relationship I was missing that caused that. In reality, what hurt was the fact that I had shut the love of my life out because of my past hurts.

I was treating God like one of my boyfriends, but He wasn't one. He is always faithful to us even when we make these past hurts our idols. The hurt controlled me for so long without my realizing it. I thought I was protecting myself, but I was basing so many decisions on my experiences instead of on God's Word.

I convinced myself I had forgiven them. When the memories would come up, I would get angry. When I would see some of the people involved, all I saw was what they had done to me. So I asked myself what I was so upset about and why it hurt me so much. Why wouldn't I just let the past go rather than bringing it up repeatedly?

The Lord whispered, "Forgiveness and love." I hadn't truly forgiven those who had hurt me, and I hid that pain in a corner of my heart, hoping it would disappear. But that attitude made me hide who it was God had called me to be.

He gave me a heart with the capacity to love zealously, but I covered it.

In my mind, I had always been a loving person who was never loved back in the right way or capacity. When we start thinking too highly of ourselves, God will show us what's really in our hearts. He revealed to me that I had no love that was pleasing to Him. My love was conditional, based on reciprocity, and hence it really wasn't love. It was more like trade by barter. "Why should I love you when you hurt me?" "Maybe if you had loved me enough not to hurt me, I would love you with everything I have."

That's not the type of love God created us for. He created us to love as He did. He loved us so much that He died for us. The whips, nails, cross, thorns, and everything else used to kill Jesus were His. Those who mocked and nailed Him were products of His breath. But He still chose to die so He could have a relationship with a broken creation that wanted nothing to do with Him. Even knowing that most people would still not love Him, He forgave them and died so they might live. That's the kind of love we were created for, not the imitation we have chosen to dwell in.

Can You See Me?

The feeling of being invisible can be very discouraging. Everyone around me seemed to be all booed up, and I was over there just trying to figure out why no one seemed to notice me. Those I liked never seemed to see me, and

I started thinking a sign on my head read, "Back Off! No Relationship Wanted!"

Of course, all those romantic movies didn't help; they seemed to further validate my incapability to attract the people I thought I wanted to attract. I even thought maybe He called me into the single ministry, but God gave me a promise one night. He whispered the time he had set apart for me, and I cleaved to it like a mother to her newborn.

When you first get a promise, it seems easier to have faith, but time often brings about doubt. We forget that time is under God's control. As the "deadline" God had given me seemed to be fast approaching, I gave into discouragement.

A group of students from my former university and I went to Tanzania for a service learning trip over spring break. During our last days, we got to explore the Safari, and it was beautiful. Unlike the regular zoo, you can't tell exactly where the animals will be, so you pretty much drive around till you find them. During this time, the Lord brought my attention to the sun, whose rays were peeking through clouds. God told me He was the soft, cuddling cloud that was hiding me. He is the cloud protecting us in certain areas of our lives because it's not yet time for the rays to shine or be seen. That has nothing to do with us but everything to do with God's plan.

You're not ugly or undesirable; you are being hidden by God until it's time for you to receive His best. Don't rush out of your season because people seem to be in the next one. Enjoy your season of singleness and the blessings it brings.

Yeah, I've heard it repeatedly too: "Enjoy your singleness." However, truly, when you look into the matter, your singleness is but for a season; it has an expiration date. There are lessons to be learned and growing that needs to take place before you can move to the next level. No one becomes the person called to love another as Christ does just by being thrown into a relationship. And as much as every woman claims to be a Proverbs 31 woman on her Instagram bio, writing it doesn't make it so; seasons of grooming and pruning whereby God molds and transforms us does. We wouldn't go into a job without some kind of knowledge, so why would we want to get into a relationship that way?

In our period of singleness, God teaches us about ourselves and shows us our hearts. When I accepted that, God showed me it wasn't necessarily the relationship or a person I wanted. I wanted the title of being someone's one and only. Deep down, I wanted to prove to everyone who had rejected me that I was worth something, to show them that the precious stone they had rejected had been taken by someone better. What a selfish reason to want to get into a relationship!

Until I dealt with my cut of rejection, I wouldn't be able to truly give my all to anyone; it would always be a competition I could never win because I'd be looking for something only God could do.

Your exes seeing you with someone else won't heal you, so move on and let God mend your heart so you can receive His best. Just like the sun, when your season of being hidden is over, the cloud of protection will open the way so your rays may be seen.

Practical Tips

- Cut off movies, music, shows, or social media sites that cause you to wallow in discontentment about your season of singleness. Guard your heart.
- Study characters in the bible who were in relationships (e.g. Abraham and Sarah), and note key lessons that can be applicable to you.
- Find people, like a local youth group or a friend, to keep you accountable and uplift you when the feeling of loneliness arises.
- Keep yourself busy! You can volunteer, join church ministries, travel, exercise, or even practice cooking skills.

Prayer

Lord, expose the contents of my heart by showing me any desire that is contrary to your word. Teach me the lessons from my past relationships, and help me to move on. Heal my heart. Fill me with your love and imprint in my spirit that you are enough for me.

Food for Thought: Power of a Relationship

During my university days, I got a great opportunity to network with various women in and outside the Christian circle. What was interesting was that the majority of our conversations focused on our relationships. Some of us settled; we knew we deserved better, but we were tired of waiting for that "better" to show up. Some had issues they hadn't dealt with, and that messed up any new relationship they entered.

From all our conversations, I began to see how much strength relationships could have on men and women alike. It appears that many spend half their lives looking for their significant others when they need to look to God, who will direct their paths. We can unknowingly put so much pressure on being in a relationship that it becomes idolatry.

> A man ought not to cover his head, since he is the image and glory of God; but woman is the glory of man. (1 Corinthians 11:7 NIV)

We were made to bring glory to God in our respective roles. We are the glory of God that was paid for with the His blood.

One of my dreams showed me how the seed of loneliness can creep in and confine us into a space God didn't intend for us. As I lay down on my bed, I saw someone lying behind me who pushed me into the wall. I tried to scream "Jesus!" but couldn't. But the more I fought, the more I was able to scream, "Jesus!" That dream was symbolic of how the things we let rule our mind affects our relationships with God. In this case, a relationship can take away from our time with God. It can wall us in and block our ability to call on the one who can save us. The emphasis we place on our significant other can overshadow God in our lives.

Yes, God did say it was not good for man to be alone, so He made woman, but He also said not to have any other gods but Him. Our God is a jealous God who has every right to be; our essence was painted in His mind, and by His breath, we gained life. He wants our attention, so when we focus so much on other things, it is easy to replace God. Whatever you place before Him becomes your idol. Set yourself free from the idolatry of people who have no breath of their own.

CHAPTER 6

The Lone Eagle

On New Year's Eve of 2013, I attended an all-night church service to usher in 2014 in the presence of the Lord. The pastor told us that when eagles fly, they don't fly in packs or pairs but solo. I chuckled. It was yet another confirmation about my "friendship situation" from God. Pretty much most of my life seemed to have been partially spent attempting to understand this condition. Sigh!

There was just something about the term *best friend* that had had me on a hunt since grammar school. I'd been born in Nigeria, and the school system was much different from the one in the States. I can't recall exactly the moment I gave the title of best friend away, but I remember my primary school bestie. We did a lot of school activities together, but when I think about it now, I don't think I really knew her that well. But hey, what did I know then? I just wanted to say I had a bestie.

When I turned nine, we grew apart. I don't remember talking to her after I graduated from primary school. Then I moved to secondary school, the equivalent of high school in America. I began a search almost immediately for a replacement best friend. I attended an all-girls' boarding school four hours from home, pretty much in the middle of nowhere with thousands of students. My search was tedious, but mere numbers weren't going to stop me.

When I found out my search wasn't working, I looked at what my peers where doing. Instead of having just one best friend, they formed a larger group of besties, and they usually had one thing in common. I lived in Lagos State and was schooled in Benin, so when I found a group of friends who for the most part lived in Lagos, I decided that was the group I wanted. I did all I could to become their friend. I shared my food, my secrets, everything! But I was never able to get into that circle, and I eventually gave up trying.

I lived my life that way for years and didn't even notice it was a problem. I always searched and tried hard, and I did end up with friends but no best friend. At least that's what I thought until I went to college, where my craving for approval and friendship led me again into some forced relationships, and you can't make anyone a friend by force. The feeling of rejection creeped in, but what I though was rejection was actually my protection. God was covering me to save me for His best.

My awakening didn't happen till I found myself on a merry-go-round of betrayal after betrayal. One day, I had had enough, and I cried out to God to please take the pain away and help me trust only Him. The scales fell off my eyes; for the first time in years, I could see again. I had been so thirsty for a bestie that I had ignored the only one who had been loyal to me through it all, Jesus. I realized the reason most of my friendships hadn't worked out was because they weren't supposed to.

I'd been mad about people not having my back or acting the way friends should, but there I was, doing this same thing to God. I thought I was such a great friend, but in reality, I was like the people I felt had hurt me. God alone was the real friend, just as He has always been. He showed me I was never alone, but He had separated me for a reason. In the space He has set aside for me, the fewer voices attempting to cloud His voice, the better it was for me. I had a tendency of listening to my friends more than I did to God.

God would call me out of certain acts of the world, and I would go back because my friend had given me justification for why it hadn't been that bad. The next time you think your friends' words are greater than His, ask them to speak into dust and see if it turns into a human being. I thought there must have been something wrong with me. I mean, why did it seem like my friendships weren't lasting and people were being pulled out of my life?

It was God protecting me from myself and the person I became when I was around certain people. He had been hiding me from disaster the whole time, and all I did was complain. I was scared to be alone because I thought that if I stayed still long enough, I would find myself.

When all the noise is gone, we have to listen to our thoughts and find out who we really are; it can be scary to discover that the people we think we are isn't real. God is light, so when He shines on the dark places, it exposes the content.

Nonetheless, we should not be afraid to be alone with God, because there is beauty in His presence. God delivers us so we can share our testimonies and maybe help just one person not make the same mistakes we have. We can be whole only when we learn to be content with God and who He made us to be. Searching for someone to complete and validate us only adds to our journey to the expected end God has for us all.

God cut off those branches for a reason, and as hard as it might seem, we have to just let go. Relationships that aren't God ordained are slow but sure death sentences.

Sometimes, even when God exposes these toxic relationships, we still choose them. I guess we prefer the poison we're familiar with.

It's the fear of uncertainty that's causes us to cleave to this death sentence rather than the abundant life God wants to give us. Winging it is uncertain, but following God's plan guarantees us an expected end. Whatever we lose in the process will be replaced by something more wonderful than we ever imagined. All the friends I thought were mine were replaced by people who were a direct reflection of God's undying love for me. Had I held on to my toxic relationships, I would have never seen clearly that God had something better in store for me.

A Way of Escape

God will create ways out for us when we find ourselves in tricky or even scandalous situations. Having a way to get out is just half the battle; we have to decide we will take it. Will we choose the way out or risk staying in that bad situation?

I once found myself right outside a party I had no business attending. God had delivered me from it for a while, but I was curious. *What would it feel like to go back into this scene? Will I enjoy myself? Maybe I can just sit in there and observe.*

The Enemy is a conman. Doubt is not of the Lord, and the fact I wrestled to make a decision about going in or not was confirmation that God didn't approve. Though I didn't hear His still voice give me the go ahead, I still almost went in, believing that I could maybe have a "cheat" day.

Some people may think you're being overly sanctimonious. Why are parties bad when you're just going there for some fun? *My intentions are good, so it's not that bad,* we may think. I definitely was the one who made fun of the "overly sanctimonious" people who I felt took Jesus way to seriously. I even joined those who labeled others who seemed too sanctimonious as "Sister Marys." That was until God tugged on my heart. He wanted to consult with me about my attitude.

For a long time, I asked God, *Is it bad that I go to parties? Should I go?* One night, I had a dream that will stick with me forever. I was in a long line in front of what looked like a judgment table. Every time I felt myself getting closer, I let people go ahead of me until I could avoid it no longer. It was my turn. I was standing in front of a judge who asked me, "You've been wondering whether to go to parties, right?"

How'd he know that?

He said, "Don't go."

I looked up to see him, but the table of judgment disappeared. I woke up.

I even tested God's patience by asking, "Can I get a couple more signs just to make sure it was really you?" In reality, I didn't need more signs. I knew God had given me one of the clearest answers I'd ever gotten.

I still went to a couple parties after that dream, but I always felt so out of place. I began to wonder why we had to dance in the darkness. *Can't we put on the light? Are we hiding? Would I dance like this if the lights were on? Would I invite Jesus to this party? Would Jesus invite me to this party? If the rapture happened right here and now, where would I be spending eternity?*

Although some of my friends didn't understand this change and thought I was being "holier than thou", the truth was that God had given me this word, not them. Why should I expect them to see it from my perspective when the word had been crafted for me in that season by God?

I knew that since God had warned me, I had to make a choice because I was going to be held accountable. It wasn't an easy choice—I love to dance, and it was a way for me to burn off stress. But God is worth more than that. He is the giver of peace, so I didn't need to look for it anywhere else.

As minor as it might seem, the subject of partying and clubbing is a very controversial topic in the church. However, I will be very transparent about the revelations I received from God about it. The atmosphere and people in those places caused me to not only compare myself to but to also try to outdo other girls. If they thought they were going to have the flyest outfit, they must have not seen me shopping for a dynamite dress I was going to wear only once to stunt on them. I know ya'll do it, so judge not lest ye be judged. I joke! I joke!

The clubbing scene subconsciously creates a rivalry in people's minds that some aren't even aware of. Let's dive into the dancing. Would you twerk in front of Jesus? Would Jesus twerk on you? For those who aren't hip on the latest club lingo, twerking is a dance that usually involves a boy and girl. The girl bends over and winds her bum all over the boy's private area. Some boys just let the girls twerk on them, but sometimes, they attempt to follow the girl's movement. What a way to invoke lustful desires! Maybe you don't see harm in it, but it could harm your partner. As members of the body of Christ, we share in the joys and sufferings of the rest. We ought to look out for their best interest and not contribute to their dysfunction.

When I use to be up in the club, winding my waist like nobody's business, I usually went with my friends and I noticed I would try to outwind some of them. I wanted to be desired, look sexy, and attract attention. It was very exhausting and unnecessary, but I did it anyway. I was on a mission to set traps for guys up and down but never deliver the goods.

Thank God for mercy. I would still be in that disheartening state thinking I was living well. I was actually in bondage and didn't know it. The music would send signals to my brain and cause me to act uncharacteristically. Sometimes, I would cuss, sexually winding my body across the dance floor, acting like the girl I heard in the song. I would try to tease guys. The songs they played planted seeds of lust and discontentment in my heart. The music, lyrics, and atmosphere drained me spiritually.

I usually went to African parties and clubs, and one thing about Africans is that they like to make grand entrances. Tell them the party starts at 10:00 p.m., and they'll stroll in at 1:00 a.m. as if they were early. That meant I wouldn't get home till about 4:00 a.m., and then it was another thirty or so minutes before I got to bed. Church started at ten in the morning, and I would be so tired. God would be speaking a word through my pastor, but I would be half asleep and missing the answers I asked for because I had chosen the world over Him. Those parties had repercussions for me physically, emotionally, and spiritually.

Even after being delivered from that poison, I was still curious about what would happen to me as I stood in front of that party years later. When I was standing in front of the door of that party I was debating going to, I realized it was a restaurant with a dance floor and thought, *It can't be that big of a deal.*

I felt such a great tug on my heart, but my curiosity was tugging at me too. I tried to justify my going in, but when you're walking in God's purpose, you don't need to justify to yourself or others why you're doing what you're doing. As I walked with some friends toward the door, remembering fully what God had told me, I saw some people walk into the party. I ducked in an attempt to bury my face in my telephone like I was on Instagram doing important things. They were people I used to hang out and party with in my "Pre-Jesus days," as some of my friends would say.

I knew at that moment that I couldn't return to the vomit I had been delivered from no matter how enticing it looked. The irony of vomit looking good is crazy, but when your eyes are veiled, even dysfunctional things can look good. When the bouncer told me it was $10 to get in, I said, "Thank you, Lord!" He knew I wasn't going to pay. There it was—my way of escape.

As I walked away with my "cheap" friends, the bouncer offered to let us in for free. At that point, I knew the Enemy was trying real hard for a reason. I thought about it, but then I realized it wasn't worth it. I left.

> "And when people escape from the wickedness of the world by knowing our Lord and Savior Jesus Christ and then get tangled up and enslaved by sin again, they are worse off than before. It would be better if they had never known the way to righteousness than to know it and then reject the command they were given to live a holy life." (2 Peter 2:20-21 NLT)

After being set free from something you thought brought you happiness, going back causes a deeper attraction to it. Even if my friends wanted to go, I shouldn't have considered it at all. My race was not their race. You might be thinking, *Well, I haven't gotten such a conviction from the Lord yet.* But I encourage you to see His face concerning this area of your life, because you can get numb to the tugging of the Holy Spirit if you get too used to shunning Him.

Pray to God to show you areas in your life that don't please Him. Pray to Him as well to give you the desire to change them. When He does show you these areas, don't let anything or anyone convince you to ignore His word. On judgment day, you alone will give an account for your decisions and your life.

Practical Tips

- Combat discontentment by immersing yourself in God's word of affirmation. Google or refer to the dictionary section in your bible to find scriptures addressing this issue. Set up reminders throughout the day with passages that speak to you.
- Write down God's promises and instructions given to you. Keep them in remembrance, so that you make decisions that support the vision.

Prayer

Lord teach me how to be content with you and not seek for satisfaction that only you can bring. Remind me that you have a plan for my life and that everyone who has left served a purpose during his or her season. Help me to be obedient to the conviction of the Holy Spirit.

CHAPTER 7

The Inconceivable World of Love

Love is one of the most difficult concepts known to us. As much as we profess to understand what it means and how to love, gray areas still exist. One of the most quoted verses of the Bible is,

> Love is patient, love is kind. It does not envy, it does not boast, it is not proud. It does not dishonor others, it is not self-seeking, it is not easily angered, it keeps no record of wrongs. Love does not delight in evil but rejoices with the truth. It always protects, always trusts, always hopes, always perseveres. Love never fails. (1 Corinthians 13:4–8 NIV)

It's much easier to recite that passage than to put it in action. How does one go about loving someone in such a pure way if he or she doesn't love you to the same degree? One day, the Lord asked me, "If I told you to give someone everything you have, and after you do, that person spits in your face, what would you do?"

I shook my head in disbelief. I got offended. I always thought of myself as someone who would give everything I had to others. But if I could think back to a time when I was the one in need and the same action wasn't reciprocated, I'd get antsy about being so gracious. *Why should I give my all to someone who would never do the same for me?*

God said I was getting offended over something I did to Him over and over. When He gave His grace and mercy to me, I took it and went back into the world. I took His gift and spat in His face. Even though He had died to redeem me, I still went back and surrendered myself to the very thing He died to save me from. Yet His love has never failed me. He never questioned blessing me. He remained faithful.

What excuse can we possibly have after hearing that? A blameless man died on a cross for a sin He hadn't committed just so He could save those who had crucified Him, whose sins He had taken on. We're not different from them, but He still loves us. Our goal should be to strive every day to die to our flesh and be like Jesus. Loving without expecting anything in return is part of this journey to becoming more like Christ.

True love is not dependent on reciprocity. If Jesus hadn't died for us, where would we be today? For that reason, we ought to forgive those who have hurt us and ourselves so we can be free to dwell in God's secret place. Jesus has shown by example that it's possible to love people who don't love us.

For the Sake of Love

> And the second is equally important: Love
> your neighbor as you love yourself. (Matthew
> 22:29 NLT)

"As you love yourself"—that means if we are unable to love ourselves, we cannot love others in the capacity God intended. It says love them as yourself, not love them as long as they love you, or love them if you'll get something in return. That might not even be your issue. Maybe you do good things for recognition.

> So when you give to the needy, do not announce
> it with trumpets, as the hypocrites do in the
> synagogues and on the streets, to be honored by
> others. Truly I tell you, they have received their
> reward in full. But when you give to the needy, do
> not let your left hand know what your right hand
> is doing, so that your giving may be in secret. Then
> your Father, who sees what is done in secret, will
> reward you. (Matthew 6:2–4 NIV)

We tend nowadays to share everything we're doing or thinking. Social media has made it so much easier for us to broadcast even private matters. But people's praise or recognition can never compare to the heavenly reward of eternal life.

Evaluation does a whole world of good especially with issues that involve motives. When we begin to examine why we give—whether time, money, effort, or love—we might be shocked to find out our reasons don't revolve around one of the most important commandments, love.

So before you make that Facebook post or announce all the community service you do, ask yourself what your reason is for sharing.

Prayer

Jesus, please reveal yourself to me by showing me what true love looks like, and how to put it into action. Forgive me if I have devalued love in anyway, cleanse my heart, and lead me to yourself. Let all my actions stem out of love without expecting anything in return.

CHAPTER 8

Public Service Announcement

After three years in junior secondary school in Nigeria, I left the all-girls' Catholic school in Benin City and moved back to Lagos State. Benin City is landlocked, and a majority of the roads are covered with rich, red soil. Benin has a long history; although it has undergone renovation, its historical sites are preserved. There are a number of tribes but less ethnic diversity there as compared to Lagos.

Lagos State, Nigeria's commercial hub, encompasses a huge coastal area that hosts loads of foreign companies, especially oil and gas, and that has attracted a huge population. Lagos State reminds me of some states in America.

However, I left Lagos when I was nine; I was eager to be grown up, so I skipped my final year of primary school and took the entrance exam to secondary school. I was surely not going for the schoolwork but for the independence. While most nine-year-olds were playing with toys or eating ice cream, I was in deserted farmland fetching buckets of water on my head by choice. I learned quickly that independence wasn't always glamorous as I thought.

The senior secondary school I attended in Lagos was much different from my school in Benin for many reasons. It was a mixed-gender school, and I could actually grow my hair. My Catholic school in Benin made all the girls cut their hair. They told us something about our being able to focus better if the breeze could reach our scalps and that we would do much better if we weren't worried about our hairstyles.

My new school wasn't as big as my former school, but at least I could see civilization instead of farmland through the gates. In my old school, which was known for quality education and training, I could have never dreamed of running away because I probably wouldn't have made it more than ten minutes down the street.

In my new school, I was exposed to a problem—boys. I knew what they were, but I had never been in a boarding school where I saw them every day. The problem was the competition among us girls for their attention. We were all trying to be noticed, but some girls got noticed way more than others. My idea of flirting was making fun of the boys, kind of elementary, but hey, that was the only method I knew.

I remember people telling the overly sanctimonious girls, who apparently included me, that we were too stiff because we refused to open ourselves to explore more with guys. One girl even told me publicly, "The only reason you're a virgin is due to lack of opportunity."

Ouch. My response was that at least I wasn't giving it out to little boys who were telling everyone on campus about it. That was my pre-Jesus response; my heart was polluted until the Lord showed me a side of myself I had never known before. I thought I was better than those girls who had lost their virginity. Yes, I agreed to do other things, but at least I hadn't lost myself. But I finally realized that just because I was a virgin didn't mean I was pure in heart. I thank Jesus for being the cure to my heart condition.

You may not be having sex, but your mind could still be polluted. You're masturbating, having sex with people in your dreams, watching pornography, rubbing up on people, having oral sex, or provocatively dancing to draw sexual attention to yourself. You are committing sins of lust even if you are not pushing your boundaries all the way. Just as a half-truth is a lie, half-purity is no purity. Sometimes, it's not even that someone out there is breaking God's heart with sin that bothers you; it's that you have the same thoughts but not the same nerve to actually commit the sin.

When I was in college, the Lord told me one day, "Sure, you're a virgin physically, but in your mind you're just as guilty as the prostitute down the street." He told me my thoughts were just as vile as those who engaged in premarital sex. I would mentally do the same with brethren I saw and think I had one over on those who physically sinned, but we both sinned, and the wages of all sin is death (Romans 6:23 KJV).

> But I tell you that anyone who looks at a woman
> lustfully has already committed adultery with her
> in his heart. (Matthew 5:28 NIV)

As explicit as my words are in this chapter, my intent is not to bash anyone but to show that purity goes way beyond sex. Our actions stem from what's in our hearts, and the more we let those thoughts simmer, the closer we get to their manifestation in our lives. Proverbs 23:7 tells us as we think, so are we, and Proverbs 4:23 says we should guard our hearts because everything we do flows from it.

The Bible states clearly that premarital sex is a sin, so I want to encourage everyone out there who struggles with this. There is a way out of this bondage, Jesus Christ. It might seem like you're missing out on something by giving it up, but you're not. God created sex to be enjoyed in the context of marriage as an expression of love. Marriage is a physical representation of the beautiful relationship between Christ and His bride, and the sex is just a perk.

Unfortunately, society has caused people to take the matrimony out of the picture and just keep the sex, not knowing sex is just a piece of a much greater package. It's like buying a cell phone but taking just the charger and leaving the phone on the counter. We have corrupted beauty. Ecclesiastes 3 tells us that there is a time for everything, a time to make love and a time to abstain. There are perks of saving ourselves for marriage whether we're virgins or celibate.

- You glorify God with your body, which means you're walking in the purpose He created for you.
- You don't have to worry about using protection and getting pregnant when you're not ready.
- You don't have to worry about contacting sexually transmitted diseases.
- You and your future spouse can enjoy the fruits of your labor with God's blessing.

- You learn perseverance and how to deny your flesh so God's Spirit can rule.
- You get the chance to know people you are in relationships better if sex isn't clouding your judgment.
- You save yourself a lot of heartache.

No matter what situation you're in, know that you are so precious in God's eyes and there is nothing He won't do for you to meet Him in paradise. You are more valuable than lustful thoughts or actions. You are a spitting image of Him. Remember when Jesus talked about the shepherd who left his ninety-nine sheep to search for one? He said that in heaven there was much more rejoicing over that one. Regardless of how far you think you've strayed from the truth, you can never outrun God's mercy. He will do whatever it takes to bring you home to Him where you belong. Jesus loves you!

Practical Tips

- We have to guard our hearts and minds against the Enemy, and just opening the door a little means we're aiding and abetting him. Those of us who struggle with lust of the eyes should think about ways they come in contact with such images; whether it's television, social media, YouTube, music, or friends, they have to make a break with whatever fuels their dysfunction.

- Seek out those who can hold you accountable to yourself, keep you in check when needed, and pray with you when you feel vulnerable.
- Even after getting rid of the sources of our lust, our memories can draw us back in; Ask God for His help in overcoming lust; spend time in His presence and create new memories to replace the old.
- Memorize helpful passages from the Bible and check in with God frequently to keep your mind focused. Focusing on the things of God can help flush out bad habits and shift your focus to good things.
- Seek out churches or ministries that help people deal with these issues.
- Pray, pray, fast, and pray! And do that some more to learn how to tame your flesh.

Prayer

Father, you know our hearts and where we have fallen short. Help us tame our flesh so we can please you. Encourage us on our path to righteousness and give us strength because on our own, we are weak. Equip us to defeat any issue of lust or sexual immorality knowing that the only person we need to please is you. Take away any pride that causes us to condemn others in sin and replace it with your everlasting love. Father, help us embrace the person and despise sin not just in their lives but also in ours.

Food for Thought: Kissed with the Moon— With Love from Tanzania

Ahh! Jesus, lover of my soul! It's amazing how time, distance, or place can't restrain God from chasing, loving, and wooing us.

As I write this, I am in Tanzania on a service learning trip, and despite the distance from America, the Lord is still jealous for every beat of my heart every second of every day.

I'm reading *Captivating* by John and Stasi Eldredge. The words are so powerful that I usually need time to let them sink in. I recommend this book for women who truly desire to unravel the true women God intended them to be.

I read some things that wrecked every bone in my body. Stasi wrote about these little kisses the Lord gives here and there just to remind us of His unending love for us. After reading it, I asked the Lord to give me a kiss I would never forget. That evening, our Tanzania team gathered to talk about the day and the next day's event. I might have been zoned out, because I couldn't stop thinking about everything I had read. It baffled me how God could still chase after a bride who had replaced Him with another groom. All of a sudden, I felt a tug on my heart to turn to my left, and there it was. The kiss I had asked God for was projecting rays of commitment and pure love toward me. The moon had never looked so beautiful. I looked at others; only I had noticed it.

The full moon shone so brightly that I didn't need a flashlight, and my heart melted. I knew God was reminding me that it didn't matter what mountains seemed to have risen between us, He was going to woo me to the ends of the earth. He was assuring me that His rays of eternal love were strong enough to lead me out of my dark place. I didn't need a flashlight or any other man-made solution to lead me; He would handle that.

CHAPTER 9

Grace

The book of Romans contains a consistent message of grace unearned, undeserved, but never ending. We are wrong if we think we can earn this grace Jesus gave His life for.

> For it is by grace you have been saved, through faith-and this is not from yourselves, it is the gift of God. (Ephesians 2:8 NIV)

Grace is a gift given by God, so why do we try to earn it? A gift bought the blood of the only righteous man, God in the flesh. No dust, no wrinkle, no blemish, but purity, uprightness, and holiness. How could we pay for grace we do not understand? A gift is no longer a gift if we earn it; it would be called wages. We sometimes treat our relationships with God as if they were nine-to-five, unemotional jobs, and we check in just occasionally about our reward.

Grace is not about us but about what Jesus did on the cross. The price was paid in full and then some, so we can't double pay. That would be like learning from a cashier at a supermarket that some good Samaritan ahead of us had paid our bill but saying, "Nah, I still want to pay for it."

We don't want to owe anyone anything; we want to be independent. But leaning on someone doesn't mean weakness, especially when that someone is God. Only the strong can lean on God because it takes strength to deny those desires to be independent and let Him work. Only the strong can admit they can't handle things on their own and need help. When Jesus died on the cross, He said it was finished, paid in full, so we don't have to pay again.

Adversity 101

Lord, why does this keep happening to me? I gave my life to you, but I'm battling. Shouldn't my life be easier now? No one wants to sign up for a life of adversity. I know life with God never seems like a straight path, and obstacles crop up, but they can build us up. It is not an easy journey, and regardless of what we think is leading us, God is in charge of our paths. Mere human love or strength could never get us out of what might seem a life-sucking situation.

In the moment of adversity, we should remember there's an end to every dark tunnel, even if that end might seem to be farther away than we would like.

I found myself in one of the most challenging situations again—being lonely. I like the company of others; I find joy in sharing moments and enjoying life with people. Toward the beginning of my senior year of college, when

God started to speak about how He was going to separate me from everything I was used to, I cried. He was requiring more of me as I entered a new season of growth. During one service, one of the choir's songs got me in tears and on my knees. God was clearly telling me He was requiring more of me. I thought that where I had come from hadn't been easy, and now He wanted more?

As much as my flesh wanted to fight it, I fell to my knees, a physical representation of surrendering my heart to God's will no matter how outrageous it seemed.

I started a job that required a lot of travel; I was away from family and friends. I thought the Lord would send me someone with whom I had something in common, but He wanted time to be alone with me. He was tired of sharing me with everyone and watching me run from Him. My loneliness drove me to tears; I felt like an outcast, a shadow in the midst of my peers.

"This is too much! I have to quit," I told the Lord.

"Trust me. I have plans for you," He said.

"Yeah, Lord, I know you do, but my life is really hard right now."

"Be still and know that I am God," He said.

My father gave me some wise words one of the many nights I was bawling my eyes out: "You may think you're the minority, but when you have God, you are actually the majority. All you need is God"

It's crazy that being different is frowned upon, especially when the differences in people's minds and backgrounds can result in creativity and originality. I couldn't be unique and fit in at the same time just as we can't be half and half with

God. Either we pursue who He called us to be or follow the world's definition of us.

No matter how much strife we meet or how uncomfortable life might seem, God's definition of us is the best there could ever be. We make the mistake of assuming God's path is adversity free; He didn't promise we wouldn't run into trouble, but He did say all things would work out for the good of those who love Him.

> "I have told you all this so that you may have peace in me. Here on earth you will have many trials and sorrows. But take heart, because I have overcome the world." (John 16:33 NLT)

In the Wilderness

At the time, I didn't realize He had called me into the wilderness so He could talk to me free from distractions. I kept yelling that I was hungry and wanted to be surrounded by the people who had always fed me—my Bible study, church, family, and friends.

He said, "I called you here so I could feed you myself. Have you forgotten how I fed the Israelites with manna? They ate and were full. I will fill you the same way. You will not go hungry because I am the Word, the manna that filled my people."

I said, "But my heart seems hesitant, unclean. It's mad at you for taking me away from everything we built together."

"I am greater than your heart," God said. "I took away everything you are familiar with because I have something much better for you. I wouldn't be able to give it to you if you were surrounded with the familiar. You would never accept that change. Don't be afraid of being with me, of dwelling in my presence. Yes, I shed light on dark places, but it's my way of pruning you so you will end up looking like me—no spot, no blemish, no wrinkle. You are my clay."

"Sometimes, I don't understand myself," I told Him. "My heart confuses me. For a long time, I've desired more. That 'more' I desperately need has been chasing me since before the foundation of the world, but it just wasn't enough. It didn't seem real. How can I make it work? Where do I start?"

"I'll lead you beside quiet streams," God told me.

He would lead me. He didn't ask me to help Him direct my footsteps. He said He would lead and I should follow. I was complaining about how He was taking me away from the people I thought were feeding me when in reality it wasn't them feeding me, it was God using them to feed me.

> Remember how the LORD your God led you all the way in the wilderness these forty years, to humble and test you in order to know what was in your heart, whether or not you would keep his commands. He humbled you, causing you to hunger and then feeding you with manna, which neither you nor your ancestors had known, to teach you that man does not live on bread alone but on every word that comes from the mouth of the LORD. (Deuteronomy 8:2–3 NIV)

Sometimes, you have to be taken to a place to become dependent on God rather than the vessels He has placed around you. Don't become so dependent on God's vessels that you forget how to depend on Him. He knew what He was doing when He took me to a place where I had no one, and it caused me to hunger.

You might be hungry because you feel by yourself, but your hunger is not a mistake; it's a God-ordained hunger. What you hunger for is the revelation of God in a new, captivating way. A vessel cannot supply itself; God supplies the vessel, so quit trying to get filled from limited sources; what they have will carry you only so far. Get filled till you overflow from the eternal source. You can stay in the space, although it seems lonely, and walk in purpose, or you can live in a façade of completion. You must choose to move to a new level with God or settle with where you are.

Some people might say, "I've chosen to go with Him since I was four!" But I've learned that choosing God is a daily decision. As His mercies are new every morning, our hearts need to be renewed in Him constantly. Sometimes, we choose Him and then forget about Him; He isn't at the forefront of our minds. When we choose Him daily, we put Him in the position to control our steps before we take them.

Every day will offer us new challenges, different scenarios, new people, different situations, and so on. That requires us to make decisions on a daily basis to let Him handle the old, the present, and the future. That's why His mercies are new every morning.

Prayer

Lord, strip me of any pride that limits me from leaning on you, reminding me that in my weakness you are strong for me. Help me to accept your grace and stop trying to earn it. Be my strength and source in the wilderness. May I renew my mind towards you daily, surrendering all that I am into your able hands.

Food for Thought: Why fight?

Even when I feel insecure, even when I repeatedly fail, I choose Him over myself because He is always there. Even after I say, "Lord, I can't be how I was anymore. I want to change. No turning back," I can find myself just seconds later right back in the filth I was trying to run away from. Nonetheless, Jesus reaches in that filth, pulls me out, and calls me His beloved child. He cleans me of the dirt I have buried myself in and declares me perfect by His blood. How could I ever give up on such an amazing God? So I stand and keep going, knowing He has such high hopes for me. I'll keep fighting; I find hope in Jesus' blood.

CHAPTER 10

Back to the Basics

Every once in a while, I feel trapped, and that's never a good feeling. I know I belong to Christ but feel I'm in a bubble. I can lose my spark for God, who can seem so far away. Someone moved. It wasn't Him; it was me who had moved. Even though I wanted to blame Him, it was me. I appeared far away, maybe even so far off that my fear convinced me I couldn't possibly get back on track. How could He give me another chance after I'd said the last time that I was in it for real? It couldn't possibly be happening again, could it? But it was. It did.

I've learned I'm never too far to turn back to God. Like the father of the Prodigal Son, His arms are constantly extended to me in hopes I'll come home. Sure, it might look bad, but the steps of the righteous are ordered by God, even the steps that look way off track. Every time my spark seemed to dwindle, God revealed Himself to me in a new way that made me fall in love with Him again.

I would start from the beginning again and reread stories about God. I even started from Genesis, and it was amazing; I received fresh revelation on what seemed like old words.

My spark came back. A passion for the heart of God was ignited once more in my soul!

The promises He made are still good. I remember reading about how God promised Noah He would not flood the earth again. The rainbows we see should remind us of how faithful God is. His Word doesn't obey time; it's the other way around. To think that is just one of the many promises that still stand shows how amazing God is.

The Irony of the Human Mind

I had an exam in one of my classes senior year in college that I had to do well on to graduate. A week before the exam, I started reviewing a couple of chapters a day, leaving me a day and a half to pull it all together. However, I did the bare minimum of studying just to be able to say I had studied.

On exam day, I told God, "Okay, let me be honest. I've been trying to deceive myself. I didn't do what I was supposed to do. Lord, I know I don't deserve this, but please be merciful this one last time and bless me with a grade I know I don't deserve."

You know how sometimes we try to play the honest card with God? Like we really aren't sorry for what we did but we want something and we know He loves honesty, so we try to use the truth to manipulate His emotions? He can read through all that; He sees our hearts no matter how crafty or clever we think we are.

I got my score on this electronic exam almost immediately. I received a B. You'd think I would have been happy, right? I hadn't really studied and had tried to manipulate God, but He was still gracious enough to give me an above-average grade. Truth is, I was upset. What I was really praying for was an A though I knew I didn't deserve it.

Some of us Christians have become so entitled that we believe we deserve every good and perfect thing when they are actually gifts from God. He has right to distribute them as He pleases because they are His. It's because of His love for us that He gives us gifts, not because we deserve them or can earn them.

So why was I mad? At whom was I mad? My teacher? God? Myself? I thought about who I could call to pour my guts out to, but I neglected the one who had been by me during my "fake" study sessions, as I was on the bus, during the exam, even when I hit the "save and submit" button. I was mentally ranting, but He gently reminded me of His presence. I was so angry He hadn't given me what I wanted that I forgot I didn't deserve it to begin with. My thoughts went quiet. My heart got sad.

How often do we fail to see that God is a righteous judge, a loving Father, and a trustworthy friend? He spoke to me throughout my studying and prompted me to study harder. But I hadn't done that because I felt He would bail me out. If believers can treat Christ that way, what makes them different from unbelievers?

We try to use God the same way unbelievers may try to manipulate people for their own benefit. Unbelievers don't claim to love God, but we claim to walk in His footsteps yet still try to manipulate Him. We rub His lamp when it's convenient; we want the gift, not the gift giver. God gives us an assignment with instructions about how to handle it, but we're too lazy to be bothered with the process; we just want the product, the prize, the gift. And then we get upset when we miss the prize God had intended for us in spite of the fact He had done His part but we hadn't done ours.

Play your part today.

Resurrecting Old Wounds

I apologize in advance if the following grosses you out, but when I was younger, I was what you could call a "picker." No, not a pickpocket; I had the nasty habit of picking at my sores and opening them up again. My mother would say, "Ufuoma, why are you resurrecting those sores? Leave them alone." We can all refuse to let our wounds heal by picking at them even when they're healing.

Maybe it's because we haven't figured how to let our sores be. It's not that we don't want them to heal; it's more a matter of our not knowing how to let them heal. We claim to surrender these wounds to God at the altar and give Him control to heal us, but then we scratch them back open the next day. In reality, we haven't given them over to God.

On November 6, 2012, I wrote a blog post entitled, "Old Ghosts Reappearing" that addressed why our problems can resurface.

> We live in a society that would much rather we shove things to the side and pretend we have dealt with our "issues" than honestly face them. After

much reflection, I concluded I hadn't really "let go" of some things I knew were holding me back. What I did, like most others do, was attempt to make my heart believe it was over the heartbreaks, anger, and desires that didn't please God and I had forgiven the people who had hurt me. I was so blinded I couldn't see that these issues I hadn't dealt with became my "ghosts" that hid in a corner of my heart and hindered me from moving forward.

How do you know if you're living with a ghost? If someone offends you and you say you have forgiven him or her but you get upset when you remember the offense, you unfortunately haven't let go. Matthew 6:15 NIV tells us, "But if you do not forgive others their sins, Your father will not forgive your sins."

When we hold on to these ghosts, we unknowingly put a halt on our relationship with God and allow ourselves to be held in mental bondage. That thing or person we let rule our minds could have moved on, but we for some reason let that issue define us. Hence, when old issues that provoked our anger, jealousy, unforgiveness, and hatred reappear, that means the ghosts never left.

These ghosts will not leave you in peace, so not letting go is a sign you have chosen to remain in captivity. The blood of Jesus has given us the ability to walk in freedom, but why do we choose to be in such slavery?

Romans 12:2 NIV says, "Do not conform to the patterns of this world, but be transformed by the renewing of your mind. Then you will be able to test and approve what God's will is—His good, pleasing and perfect will."

We are to serve a God who is bigger than any issue. If only we would go to Him in prayer and sincerely ask Him to change our hearts. Jeremiah 17:9 tells us that the heart of man is desperately wicked, and no one can understand it. God knows why we act the way we do because He can search our hearts.

As people of God, we need to do whatever it takes, especially in these times, when the signs are clear that Christ is soon to come. If it takes praying every day for God to strengthen us to overcome our sinful natures, let's do that.

I serve a God who can look beyond my nature to hold onto things I know won't prosper me. He loves us, and He is willing to help us be free as long as we are willing to come into His presence with sincere hearts.

All this is to say we're going about this battle the wrong way. Cutting off a branch will not erase the problem; killing the entire tree from the roots will. Branches can grow back once they're cut off, but when you kill the tree at its source, you can replant a new one from seed. We haven't dealt with an issue if we barely dusted the surface but neglected the issue that is deeper than the visible wound.

I picked on my sores to avoid dealing with whatever issue I was facing; it was my coping mechanism. The reason we let our ghosts live on is because the branches look less intimidating that the roots. If we convince ourselves that our problems are just on the surface, like a sore, we don't have to dig deeper to the real reason we are the way we are.

God wants us to be free, and although the roots look intimidating, remember that we do not work by sight. Goliath looked intimidating, but you know what brought him down. God can do anything. He wants us to be free, so we should let Him truly heal us so we can move on in our journeys.

Jailed

Every time I saw or heard of you, I pictured you in a cell, behind bars. I laughed because karma had caught up with you. Then God pushed me back into reality. My mind was playing tricks on me, telling me my anger had put you behind bars when it was really me behind those bars. The Enemy taunted me with a reflection of you walking freely on the other side, mocking me for thinking I could hold you bound. Knowing the truth doesn't always make things easier; I know this because knowing what I knew, I still held on to this anger tighter than a pinky promise. I wasn't letting go. How could I?

How could I let it go after what you had done to me? You tormented me every day; you plotted to take me out and turn my home into a house. A very sad one at that. The streets sounded so much warmer, and some days, I wished I could be there instead.

My mind was never the same. I wept to God to explain how I had ended up in this Cinderella like story but with no happy ending. No prince, no apology, just more lies and hate from someone about whom the only thing I knew was her name.

I shouldn't have been surprised. The moment she stepped foot in my home, I knew something was off. My spirit was unsettled and tears rolled down my face because I knew evil had just walked in. But no one was going to listen to me; I was but a child in their eyes, and the more I tried to rebel, the further I was pushed behind enemy lines, a very lonely and cold place. Every moment I spent there increased my hate for her. As the hate grew stronger, the more my anger rose, but it didn't stop there. Hate brought along its friend, unforgiveness.

The Lord told me I was holding on to unforgiveness, and I said I wasn't because I choked up my feelings and buried them deep in my heart and held up a banner that read, "I have forgiven." I said I had forgiven you, but they were just words. God saw my heart; He can read past all the tales we tell to disguise our hurt.

As much as you want to believe that staying angry at someone will keep him or her in a cell, you are the one who is in bondage. Forgiveness doesn't mean just letting them go; it means receiving the freedom that Jesus paid for with His blood.

God has a plan, but that darkness you harbor cannot dwell in His presence. As much as you would like to believe they put you behind those bars, you did it to yourself. Everyone has a choice, and unfortunately, you chose wrong. The moment I chose to deliver a piece of my mind to the Enemy instead of giving it to God, I chose wrongly.

> In your anger do not sin Do not let the sun go down while you are still angry, and do not give the devil a foothold. (Ephesians 4:26–27 NIV)

The Bible doesn't deny us the right to be justly annoyed, but it cautions us to not dwell. When we let in even one demon, it will never be satisfied until it has destroyed us. We should never give the Enemy a foothold over our lives or aid and abet the seed of anger because it will bear fruit. The more we tolerate it, the deeper its roots will sink into our hearts.

I ignored the issue and continued to pursue my dream of going around the world to share the gospel and let people know how amazing God is. I wanted to be a vessel by which captives were set free. But how could I do that when my vessel needed to be set free itself?

You can't set captives free when you are also a captive. How can the bound know how to unbind? If they knew and believed, they wouldn't be bound.

So here's my release to you who sought my life. I have asked God to help me forgive, but if I say I've forgotten or completely healed, I'd be a liar. Whenever I remember my pain or see your face, I asked God to remind me you were just a piece of a puzzle that maps out the redemption of a guilty woman acquitted by the mighty King.

I can't hold anything against you, because I have a debt of my own I could never repay, but I've been forgiven. All I owed has been erased, not at my plea for forgiveness but at His cross of mercy. Jesus paid the price and gave me a new slate. By His strength, my heart releases you and thanks you. Because of what happened, I got a chance to grow a branch from the seed of love that God planted in my heart. It's a branch that keeps no record of wrongs. Even without your asking for it, I forgive you because Jesus paid the price for all of us.

The Way I Said His Name

At times when I can't find the words to express the heaviness in my heart, all I have to is say one word—Jesus. God hears our silent cries. He understands just as a parent does how His children feel by just the looks on their faces.

Some days, my "Jesus" meant, "I praise you Lord. I worship you for all you have done and who you are." Some days, it meant, "Lord, my heart is weak. I need your presence, your breath. I'm lost and confused, so please save me."

In those times when my heart cried, I began to long for something more. I prayed, "Lord, there has to be more to life than this."

He responded, "Yes, my daughter, there is more. I am the more your soul longs for. You're not satisfied by this world because eternity is what I created you for, and you're just passing through this world."

God is so in tune with our hearts that He knows our hidden cries even when we can't find the words to express them. Have you ever felt a yearning but didn't know for what? If you are in that season now, lay it all out before God and listen. It's okay not to know everything; if you did, you wouldn't need God. Don't think God can't understand your longing just because you can't; nothing is hidden from Him.

> Nothing in all creation is hidden from God's sight. Everything is uncovered and laid bare before the eyes of him to whom we must give account. (Hebrews 4:13 KJV)

He knows your words before you speak them. He understands what you need before you know you need it. We live in times when some Christians condemn people for not being vocal about their prayers all the time, for not praising loud enough, for not jumping high enough. We forget that God looks at our hearts; our praise might be the loudest, but that doesn't mean it's acceptable to Him. Look at Cain and Abel. It wasn't the quantity God was looking at; it was the quality and purity of their sacrifices to Him.

When I call on His name, I mean it with everything in me. Sure, it's not an elaborate prayer, but He hears the sincerity in my plea for Him to take over. Even if you don't have any words, just go into His presence and wait in expectation. He sees your heart, so don't give up. Jesus will meet you right where you are.

Practical tips

- In a space where you feel like you can't hear God's voice or don't have a sense of direction, don't give up. If you don't know what to study, download devotionals and read Christian self-help books that encourage you to be steadfast. Take notes of the lessons you learnt and review them often. It helps in fueling your spirit man.
- Repent of any distance you might have created and seek God's face in prayer, reminding him of all the promises he made to stand by you. Again, be persistent in prayer!
- Are you lacking motivation to do your part? Philippians 2:13 shows us that God can change our desire and give us strength to do His will. Pray according to his word.

Prayer

Thank you Lord for always being consistent, even when I move away from you. Forgive me for feeling entitled to the gifts you freely give and teach me to be appreciative. Renew my mind and heal my wounded heart. Help me to forgive those who have hurt me, knowing that I'm just as guilty as them but you forgave me anyway. Search my heart Lord. Remove anything that does not resemble you.

CHAPTER 11

Faith

When God sends us on an assignment or gives us a promise, we want to see a layout of the plan. I've learned that His path is like an ocean into which you dive first and look for direction later. A GPS device, for example, takes us one step at a time; when we're approaching a turn, it lets us know. We learn to trust it's leading us the right way even when it's silent.

Faith is letting go of your willpower and taking a leap, believing God is in control of where you will land. It's surrendering your ideas of how you think things should go and clinging to God's way. Sometimes, it means letting go of the thoughts that constantly ring in your mind and tug on your heart. It means resting on the assurance that God is above your mind and heart. You have to listen to that still, small voice in your spirit that says to move in a certain way even if it's different from everyone else's or your own idea of what it should be.

Jesus looked ahead and saw a generation whose members would be taught to trust their hearts over anything when in fact the heart can be deceptive. The world teaches us we are the authors of our own stories, our own lives when even we live on borrowed breath.

Thankfully, God made a way of escape for those who are trapped by this mentality. He asks us to have faith as small as a mustard seed. Believing causes shaking in the earth and changes in heaven no matter the belief's size. No matter how much junk you've grown accustomed to, never doubt the number of mountains God will climb to get to you exactly where you are. Faith has nothing to do with present certainty but with a peace that rests on the assurance of the future.

Taking A Leap

I began officially writing this book in 2013, not knowing where it would take me. All I knew was that God gave me a promise, and within that was a book project. I didn't know its title or even its content, but I began the project and saved the file as "book" on my laptop. Doubts taunted me some nights. *How am I supposed to know how to start, God, if you won't give me specifics?*

At that time, I had been healed of a heart murmur, heartache, depression, suicidal thoughts, and much more. I held on to the promise and God's track record in my life. I held on to His faithfulness; I reminded myself He was the same yesterday, today, and forever. That thought kept me going during those times I wanted to give up.

When God gives us a promise, what are the first steps we take? Usually, we write it down to spell it out or create a picture in our minds of the promise. The Devil knows this and uses our need to see to derail us. He distorts our vision by replacing it with something else. It might not even mean the whole plan changed; he may change just little things here and there, but they can still alter our paths and confuse us.

My vision zoomed into this piece of the blueprint of my life, but the overall picture appeared hazy. God reminded me He had given me the precious gift of hope. Write the vision and make it plain, yes, but whose "plain" is it? The Enemy might try to convince you that altering the vision a little will make it more possible, but that's a lie. God doesn't lie; everything He promises will happen. Behind your Goliath is your promise, and no matter how intimidating he looks, he can never be greater than God. The fact that it seems he is blocking it cannot erase the Word of God spoken over your predestined life.

> As the rain and the snow come down from heaven, and do not return to it without watering the earth and making it bud and flourish, so that it yields seed for the sower and bread for the eater, so is my word that goes out from my mouth: It will not return to me empty, but will accomplish what I desire and achieve the purpose for which I sent it. (Isaiah 55:10–11 NIV)

The Bible says it's impossible to please the Lord without faith. When we lack faith in God, we can diminish His ability to intervene in our lives. Our faith in Him creates an avenue for Him to gain the glory in whatever situation we face. Those without faith cannot trust in God; they can be so preoccupied with their Goliaths that they ignore everything God has said and wallow in defeat. When discouraging thoughts enter your mind, conquer them with the truth of God.

It wasn't until October 2014 that the Lord spoke to me about how He would release this book. The process was not easy; at times, I'd shut my laptop for days, weeks, or even months because I was mad at God. However, He showed me my heart during those times and how rude and prideful I was being when I wasn't getting my way.

Sure, I got rejected by publishers, and just when it seemed to be going well, everything collapsed. But that didn't mean what God said was a lie. My faith wasn't withstanding the test of time because I was double minded, and we know double mindedness makes us unstable. Today I believe, but tomorrow I'm mad at God? You cannot say you serve God halfway; you serve Him completely or not at all.

When Peter stepped out onto the water, he had to forsake his friends, his boat, everything he was familiar with to do what seemed impossible. As long as you stay on the boat, you will never walk over your impossibility. You'll be like Peter's friends in the boat, a spectator rather than someone who has a personal experience with God. Choose to walk over your sea of impossibility today.

Practical Tips

- If you don't have an exact vision (project/mission) yet, ask God in prayer. When you get your vision, write it down exactly how God revealed it to you whether you understand or not. Then ask God for direction.
- Maybe your vision has to do with writing a book, starting a company or even building a local church, do your research about that area. Read books, google success stories, speak to people who have done similar things, or attend seminars/conferences. Take your findings to God in prayer and he will direct you on the next step.
- Trying to rush ahead to step-three when you barely finished step-one will overwhelm you. Pace yourself, and complete one task before moving on to another except the Lord instructs you to work on two things simultaneously.
- Whatever you do, don't alter the original plan God gave you! He doesn't need help to simplify it so it's faster or appears "easier" to accomplish. Don't be discouraged by time, and encourage yourself that even if no one has done it before, God's word will never return to him void.

Prayer

You are able to do all things including every promise and vision you have revealed to us. Let us walk in the assurance that our hope in you will never fail. Give me strength to press on when I feel like giving up. Forgive me if I doubted your power. When I am weak, please be strong on my behalf and cause me to soar on the wings of your grace. Father, give me enough faith to carry me to the finish line no matter how far it might appear.

CHAPTER 12

Worship in Spirit and in Truth

I had been thinking for a while about what worship was and what it means to truly worship God. Was it singing? Jumping? Running? Dancing? I always tried to quantify my worship based on what I saw that appeared to be worship. I tried to sing as well as the next person in hopes that God would love me as much as He loved that other person. Time after time, the Enemy would tell me that if I couldn't worship with the same intensity as the next person, my efforts would be useless, so why try? He'd tell me my life wasn't as together as those of my fellow brethren, so God couldn't possibly accept such a pathetic worship.

If you give the Enemy that proverbial inch, he'll take the proverbial mile. That con artist will creep into your mind, pollute your thoughts, and try to take control of you.

Let's first clear up this notion that there's only one right type of worship; it's not true. Yeah, I won't deny that there is worship God won't accept; it's the insincere, self-centered, people-pleasing, and manipulative type of worship.

However, declaring there's only one right way to worship puts us in a box and causes us to worship with limitations.

It's an attempt to keep us in bondage to a standard we were not created to meet. We were uniquely molded by God, so every freckle, uneven body part, deformity, or whatever was due to God's perfect will.

For so long I was kept in that box of constraint, but thank God for grace! He showed me those thoughts distracted me from what real worship is about. We were made unique, so our worship should be unique, not the same as the next person's. Why would God make us unique but want the same type of worship?

It's a mistake to think that if we don't feel excitement when we worship we aren't worshipping God. We shouldn't compare ourselves with those who look like they're feeling the Holy Spirit in them. Sure, sometimes we feel the presence of God in us strongly, but we shouldn't limit our worship to feelings because they're temporal. We won't always feel that sensation, but it shouldn't stop us from worshipping God. We're trying to get the flesh excited about the things of the spirit, when we know they're always at war.

You are to worship in Spirit not based on how your body, your flesh, is feeling, especially because it hates the Spirit. Don't try to feed your flesh worship that was made for God. I can't tell you exactly how He wants you to worship Him, but I know He wants you to use everything you are made of to bring glory to Him, so let your life be worship unto Him. Use every breath, step, word, dance, bill paid off, debt acquired—I mean everything—to worship Him. The Lord isn't in it for just the good times; He wants it all!

Whether your voice is like Whitney Houston's or not, embrace the voice God has given you and sing to Him. My cousin told me about a pastor who listened to a choir and thought, *This choir is out of tune.* God told him, *What is it to you? I like it. Don't curse what I've kissed.*

He kissed your worship beauty. To the world, it may sound like noise, but to God, it's a harmonious melody. You were created in His image and likeness, so your voice, your dance, your gifts are no mistakes. He wants you to give Him everything you are, no restrictions. The Bible tells you to worship God in spirit and in truth, so you can't say you're worshipping Him while you're simply mimicking another's praise. Embrace yourself and worship Him in truth.

Social-Idol-Media

I love that God has a sense of humor; it keeps our relationship interesting. In November 2013, I was blessed to be able to lead a Bible study at school, my first time ever, and it was about limitations. It was about how anything or anyone we place before God is an idol—family, friends, school, work; the list goes on. The whole time I was studying for that word, I never thoroughly checked myself, but God started working on me.

When the New Year came, I didn't post "New Year, new me" on my social media page, but it didn't change the fact that when we start a new season, we should take inventory. What I found I was lacking was a sold-out heart for Jesus.

There are really only two options when it comes to serving God—you're in or you're not, no middle ground.

After some reflection on why I wasn't giving my all to God, I discovered I had some idols of my own, yeah, the same idols I led the Bible study about. I'm sure you're familiar with them: Facebook, Twitter, Instagram, Pinterest, and Snapchat. It was easier to let others know their addictions to social media than to accept I needed some therapy myself. So here it goes: "Hi, everyone. My name is Michelle, and I'm a social media addict."

Admitting we have an issue is the first step, and no matter how small that step seems, it's one less step we'll need to take in the recovery process. The trap we fall into is becoming desensitized to the things that harm our walk with God. Just because something doesn't necessarily harm us at contact doesn't mean it's not slowly but surely paving the way to our destruction. We should not fall into the trap of underestimating the Enemy and the length he will go to get us to spend eternity with him.

We tend to assume just because it's not something obviously wrong like a drug addiction, it cannot be that bad. But anything we place above God is our master. From the beginning, God warned us He would not share us; He was jealous of us.

Social media increased the level of communication and created fast networking channels for people. But just like with the tree in the garden of Eden, the Enemy is trying to deceive us and manipulate its purpose.

I'm an early morning person, and starting my day out in His presence is awesome. However, at times, I found it more pleasurable to check my social media accounts. I would try to deceive myself by reading passages fast, but we can never deceive God. He knows when we're checking in on social media more than checking in with Him. Do you give God more "hits" than you give your social media?

I found myself too attracted to my social media and less attracted to the Word. I prayed, "Lord, take it away." But what's the use of praying for deliverance from such distractions if, after He delivers you, you turn right around and embrace the very thing that held you in bondage again? You're saying, "Lord, I was just kidding." Proverbs 26:11 tells us only a fool would return to his vomit.

You can be emancipated, but because slavery is your norm, you're more comfortable in that state. The familiar can grip you so tight that it could take you forty years of walking in circles to break free.

We all long to be in control, but only one person at a time can have supreme control over our lives. If we're in control, then God is at best in second place. That's not up to His standards. He wants to give us everything good and perfect, but too often we settle for less.

I signed off. Of what use is social media if the one I need to reach, the one who guarantees me freedom, is out of the picture?

Sign off the dysfunctional merry-go-round of idolatry.

Practical Tips

- Take occasional breaks from social media and this could be done in form of a fast. Sign out, delete the apps, deactivate your account, and replace it with something that will help draw you closer to God, like a devotional app.

- Temptations can come when our body is accustomed to certain acts, and it might seem impossible but fasting can help break those chains. Fasting teaches us how to deny our flesh, and opens our vessels for God to fill us up with himself.
- Use the word of God to combat any desire that rises up against the knowledge God has given you pertaining to an area of limitation.

Prayer

I rebuke every demon that tries to desensitize me and keep me from spending eternity with God in Jesus' name. He cannot have me, because I belong to you, Lord. Give me the strength to let go of those things that entangle me and cleave to your way.

CHAPTER 13

Who Authorized Your Order?

I love to converse with people. I've been that way for as long as I can remember, but I've learned to be a lot more careful because God wants my words to be used for His glory. Before, I said whatever I wanted to, sometimes the first thing that popped into my head, but now, I realize God wants me to use my gift of speaking He gave me.

It can seem all gravy to know God wants to use you in an area you love. But the dilemma comes when you struggle with letting go of the old ways of doing things and submitting to the Holy Spirit. That means speaking under His unction, moving when He instructs, and not doing things how you usually did before. You have to carry out the Lord's instructions exactly how he gave it. You can pick up habits before you dedicate yourself to God that can make the process hard. When you've been so used to a certain way of life, anything new seems weird or even impossible. That's the trick of the Enemy.

We have to lay our wills down and pick His up if we want to walk as He wants us to. I learned the hard way that God always has a reason for what He says. Once, He gave me a word for some of my friends, and after I spoke, I just kept going and going. Even after hearing Him say, "Okay, it's done. It's finished. Keep it moving!" I still had things I wanted to say, but that drains people and could even take away from the anointing in the Word that comes from heaven. Whatever gift God has given us is meant for others and to bring glory to God, not us.

He's told us that if we love Him, we should obey His commands. So how can we say we love Him if we disregard His commands and do whatever feels good? Acting like God's Word is not the same as living it. We can profess our love for Him, but really, we want to feel like we're in His will. There's a difference between living in His will and living in what we think His will is or what we wish it could be. We should evaluate the path we're on and ask ourselves, "Who is authorizing my orders?"

Prayer

Lord, thank you for all the plans you have for my life, and for putting your gifts in me. Sometimes, I want to combine your will with mine even when I know I shouldn't. The word says you are our teacher, so teach me to be obedient to your instructions and rest on your word. Search me and show me ways I have put my will above you. Give me a humble and attentive spirit, so that I may do your will.

CHAPTER 14

Jingle Bells, Jingle Bells

One night, I received a text message and a picture of a Christmas tree with these words written on it from Jeremiah 10:3–4 NIV.

> For the practices of the peoples are worthless;
> They cut a tree out of the forest,
> And a craftsman shapes it with his chisel.
> They adorn it with silver and gold;
> They fasten it with hammer and nails
> So it will not totter.

I wanted to read the whole verse to get a proper understanding of it so I wouldn't take the words out of context. After much conviction by the Holy Spirit, I decided to not rush to conclusions but try to get the background before commenting. I read the Scripture, and the next verse hit me hard.

> Like a scarecrow in a cucumber field, Their idols cannot speak, They must be carried because they

cannot walk. Do not fear them; They can do no harm Nor can they do any good.

This was a word from God to Jeremiah for His people regarding idols. Thousands of years ago, He predicted the heart of man in this generation. God showed me that some of us have begun to worship our idols and lifeless things such as Christmas trees and presents more than we do Him. We use seasons, particularly Christmas, to celebrate ourselves rather than Him. He becomes an excuse to give and receive presents. How many people actually offer gifts to Jesus during this time meant to celebrate Him?

Our birthdays are about us, of course, so His should be about Him. How would you feel if your friends said they threw you a birthday party with tons of gifts and food but forgot to invite you and kept the gifts? There's nothing wrong with making others happy and blessing them during that period, but we shouldn't give trees and gifts more attention than we do Jesus, our King. He deserves every bit of our worship every day. Let's not get so programmed that we forget the reason, not just for the season, but for life itself.

Prayer

Father, rid me of any idol I have put before you and forgive me for breaking your commandment. Teach me to not be so consumed by earthly things and focus on you, not just during special seasons but every day of my life.

CHAPTER 15

Your Legacy

I've watched the movie *Lone Survivor* like twice, and each time, it felt like my heart just couldn't take what I saw. The movie focuses on some men sent to Afghanistan to track down the leader and members of the Taliban. They were regular human beings, but they had taken an oath to protect and serve their country. They selflessly persisted despite being wounded; they chose to fight even if it meant dying.

What hurt the most was when God revealed that some people sacrifice their lives for others but do so without knowing Jesus Christ as their personal Lord and Savior and miss out on eternity with Him. I wholeheartedly love and respect all the people in the armed forces; I'm mentioning this movie just as an illustration of the fights we get into in our lives.

Wouldn't it suck to get a legacy down here but end up in hell? That would make our legacies, no matter how wonderful and self-sacrificing, of no use to us after we've gone.

We can be so earthly minded and fight so hard to be remembered that we can forget that without Jesus, whatever victory we've won won't matter in the end because we will miss out on heaven. The builder in Psalm 127 labored in vain because his foundation was not God. The Bible tells us he did indeed labor, but in the end, that didn't matter because he missed the most important foundation stone, Jesus. On judgment day, God will not recognize such laborers as His.

So what is the foundation for the legacy you want to leave on earth? Is it fueled by your will, or is it based on God's plan for you to bring Him glory? Do you imagine your fight ending in earthly or heavenly glory? Be honest. Evaluate the motive behind your fight.

Strive to leave a legacy that shows how a mighty God chose you to demonstrate His glory on earth. Your legacy should echo the perfect plan of God to lead His children into His arms for eternity.

Prayer

You know every motive in my heart and see things that I am not aware of or try to conceal. Lord, please reveal any selfish desires in me and help me keep my focus on you. Let my life be a light that bears witness of your glory to the world.

CONCLUSION

For so long, I chased admirers and desired to be loved by all. My mission was to be loved widely, but that caused me to ignore a much greater love, God's love. He loves us so deeply—beyond limits, beyond restrictions, beyond ourselves. If we were to combine the love of everyone, it wouldn't match even half of God's love for us. His love is unending; it never withers. My mind cannot comprehend why He would love such a flawed human being as me so much. Lord, have you seen my heart? I can be inconsistent, hateful, prideful, and unlovable.

But in the midst of my assessment, the Lord redirects my focus. Every time I take my eyes off Him to look at myself, my flaws become more vivid. Like Peter, when I keep my eyes on Him, I can walk even on waves, but when I take my eyes off Him, I sink. My problems swallow me, but God is mighty to save. He reaches into our oceans of worries and pulls us out with His loving hand. Yes, He is a righteous judge, so He will correct us for doubting. But my mind focuses on the fact that He saves me even when He doesn't have to.

So why does he pursue me and you? It's because we were made to bring glory to Him, and that's why He is jealous for all of us. We are all the glory of the only God. When trials and temptation are thrown at us, it's because the enemy is jealous of the depth of love God has for us that even when we rejected Him, He still gave Himself up for us. We don't need a job, relationships, millions of friends, or material things to feel loved because we are loved deeply by the one whose words hold the stars in the sky. We are loved infinitely, so much so that every issue on earth has an expiration date and will work out because we love God. Every detail of our lives has been orchestrated to lead us to our expected end in Christ Jesus.

This was one of the hardest things I had to write; it required me to be transparent and accept things about myself I had been battling with. I asked God why I needed to put my life on the front line for everyone in the world to see. What if they didn't like it? What if they didn't understand me or even condemned me? However, I realized I was telling God that others' perceptions of me was more important than His perception of me. I wanted the world to see me in a certain light so I would look better than I was. But Luke 12:4–5 tells us not to be afraid of those who can only kill the body but the one who can do that and also send us to hell. We must stop giving fear that belongs to God to man.

Don't be afraid or ashamed to share your story. Philippians 1:29 reminds us that it is a privilege to trust and suffer on behalf of God, so don't let the Enemy silence your witness. There is purpose for your pain. The apostle Paul said it best in 2 Timothy 1:11–12 NIV.

And of this gospel I was appointed a Herald and an Apostle and a teacher. That is why I am suffering as I am. Yet this is no cause for shame, because I know whom I have believed, and I am convinced that he is able to guard what I have entrusted to him until that day.

Everything you face is part of God's plan to lead you to Him. Choose to learn the lesson no matter how painful it is because the end product of pruning is the harvest. Believe that the one you have put your trust in can keep you until He comes back for you. Yes, He is coming back to take you to a land where there is no more pain, sorrow, pruning, or death. A land where His glory serves as the only source of light, and the moon is like a myth. You will walk with Him day in and day out as you were supposed to in the land of love. He is coming back for you, so hang in there and trust His plan because eternity with Him is worth fighting for.

ACKNOWLEDGMENTS

To Jesus: I want to thank you, Lord for being awesome! None of this would have been possible without your putting this vision in me. Despite my doubts and fears, you chose to use me; I am ever grateful for your patience and love.

To my father and mother: Thank you for your support, prayers, and encouragement throughout this process and for standing by me even when you didn't understand. You trusted God's plan for my life. I love you both, and I pray that God's face shines on you all the days of your life.

To my brother: I appreciate your being a listening ear and always looking out for your baby sister no matter what. I pray for God's best in your future and His covering in everything you touch. Love you!

To Zino: Thank you (and the family) for your support throughout the times I wanted to throw in the towel and for allowing God to use you to speak words of confirmation and affirmation. I pray for nothing less than God's best for your life. Lots of love, your favorite cousin.

To Nana and Ijea, my 213 crew, and home "guhs": Thank you for your support, assistance, and prayers throughout this process and beyond. Much love and every seed you've sown in my life will be multiplied in yours in Jesus' name!

To Dymonica: Neek Neek! Thank you for your constant support from back when I first knew I was going to write a book. Your assistance with this book is much appreciated, and I know God will reward you many times over!

To my Publisher: I appreciate the team at WestBow Press for helping me to bring this vision to life. May God bless you all for the work you do!

To all my family and friends who supported me through the process and encouraged me to follow the vision God gave me: I love and appreciate you all!

To everyone who believed enough to purchase this book: I thank you and pray that through it, you will hear words straight from the throne room of heaven, amen!